NEW

*PUTTING ON CHRIST
AND FINDING OURSELVES*

CLOTHES

JOHN NEWTON

Morehouse Publishing
NEW YORK · HARRISBURG · DENVER

Morehouse Publishing
4785 Linglestown Road, Suite 101
Harrisburg, PA 17112

Morehouse Publishing
19 East 34th Street
New York, NY 10016

Morehouse Publishing is an imprint of Church Publishing Incorporated.
www.churchpublishing.org

Cover design by Laurie Klein Westhafer
Typeset by Denise Hoff

Library of Congress Cataloging-in-Publication Data

A catalog record of this book is available from the Library of Congress.

ISBN-13: 978-0-8192-2903-8 (pbk.)
ISBN-13: 978-0-8192-2904-5 (ebook)

Printed in the United States of America

Dedication

To my bride, Emily: *timshel*

Contents

Acknowledgments

I offer my deepest appreciation to the team at Church Publishing and especially to Sharon Pearson. Thank you for believing in this book and for your consistent encouragement and your invaluable feedback. I am also indebted to the many authors that have "explained the Way of God to [me] more accurately" (Acts 18:26). Among them are C. S. Lewis, Dallas Willard, Tim Keller (his books *and* sermons), N. T. Wright, Eugene Peterson, John Stott, Thomas Merton, and Henri Nouwen. I am also indebted to Jim Herrington, Trisha Taylor, and Steve Capper for writing the "Faithwalking" material that has changed how I think about discipleship. I would like to thank Justin Christopher for his feedback on the first few chapters of this manuscript. But I am especially grateful for Patrick Hall. Your feedback and support throughout the writing of this book has been invaluable.

I would also like to express my deep gratitude for the Episcopal Diocese of Texas. I am blessed to work with incredible colleagues day in and day out. This book flows from the deep conversations I have had with them and from the meaningful work we engage in together.

Finally, I am grateful for my family. Emily, you are my best friend. No one has taught me more about grace than you have. Dad, thank you for teaching me how to walk on my hands. Your name is most certainly in the book.

Introduction

I once listened to a radio show that interviewed an extreme skier who had successfully escaped the experience of being buried in an avalanche. He painted a gripping picture of the cold darkness that enveloped him and the fear he experienced that his life was coming to an end. "But by the grace of God," he said, "I was able to remain calm and think."

I remember my kneejerk reaction to his statement. "In such a moment of crises," I wondered, "who has time to *think?!*" My instinct would have been to claw and crawl with every fiber of my being in a panicky attempt to free myself from the darkness. As the interview proceeded, however, I quickly learned that my first instinct would have been completely wrong. Remaining calm and thinking was precisely what was called for.

"When you get buried in an avalanche," he said, "scrambling to free yourself is usually deadly." He then explained that what *did matter* was discerning the correct direction in which to climb. This skier could have climbed in four different directions, only one of which would have led him to oxygen. The other three directions would have left him buried even deeper in the snow, with less time and less breath. In this particular instance he needed to completely "turn around" before beginning to climb. But by the grace of God he was able to remain calm and think.

I return to this interview often in my mind because it strikes me as a fitting illustration of where so many of us find ourselves.

We are enveloped in a world that buries us in promises it can't make good on. Life at times feels like an avalanche of depression or business or busyness or debt or a relationship that isn't working. Our first instinct is to climb out. What's most needed, however, is grace to remain calm and to think. What we need, more than anything, is to see the proper *direction*.

A lot of us use "religion" as our compass and obviously, as a professional minister, I think one could do much worse. But even religion, and sometimes *especially religion,* can leave us baffled, suffocated, and cold. We climb, climb, and keep climbing and it never seems to be enough.

I write this book for the "buried," whether they consider themselves religious or irreligious. What makes religious and irreligious folk different is that they often climb in different directions. What makes them remarkably similar is that they both often climb in the wrong direction. I say this from a deep conviction that to climb at all *is* the wrong direction. The Christian Gospel, after all, is not a moral lesson on how we might climb out of the darkness. It's a true Story about how God, in the person of Jesus Christ, became small and climbed *into the darkness of our world* so that He might rescue us from the avalanche. Traditionally, Christians have referred to God's rescuing work as *salvation.*

The primary metaphor I play with to expound upon "so great a salvation" (Heb 2:3) is the Biblical image of *new clothes.* We who put our faith in Christ have already been clothed with the garment of salvation. Our problem is that the garment of salvation doesn't fit. Hence the cover of this book is a child wearing shoes that would be too big for Shaquille O'Neal. We *already have* the free garment of salvation, but the "shoe doesn't fit." And until the direction of our life shifts and our desire becomes to *grow into* that splendid garment, we will continue to dress ourselves in loincloths of our own making, and thus remain buried and cold in the dark.

That's why this book is really about spiritual growth; a paradoxical and mysterious grace-driven process of coming to embody in our lives what already *is*. In speaking of spiritual growth in this way, I make three key assumptions. First, Christianity is not primarily a strategy on how to climb out of whatever mess we are in. I assume first and foremost the "good news" that we have a Rescuer who already has done that for us. Second, *only as* God gives us eyes to see that "He has rescued us from the power of darkness and transferred us into the kingdom of his beloved Son" (Col 1:13) will we find a new and empowering direction for our lives. Third, the meaning of life and the "end game" of spiritual growth are to be transformed completely from the inside out so that Jesus' life, power, and presence are channeled through us more and more and more. This transformation is the "direction" to which all creation points. Wisdom is about "aligning" our lives with the direction to which all of creation is heading.

It is important that you hear me state from the outset that spiritual growth is not something *we* do. This is so hard for us to hear because we live in a world that places a premium on being productive. It is common to assume that God also needs us to be spiritually productive. However, I am convinced that our need to achieve and produce—whether that is in the world or in our spiritual lives—comes primarily from a place of *fear and pride*. I believe that our great spiritual problem is that we are terrified we have no value and so we try and *produce it*. All frantic drives to climb are attempts to justify ourselves. Such is why we make our life about achieving, keeping people happy, making money, or staying comfortable. Like the story of Babel, we build not a tower but *an image* we think the world will accept and we make our life about refining that image. We become people-pleasers or cynics or perhaps really, really "religious." All the while we say subconsciously what the builders of Babel did—"Let us make a name for *ourselves*" (Gen 11:4, italics mine). Our great fear is that if we do not make a name for ourselves—by being a funny person or a successful person or a likable person or a strong person—we might just get left behind in the avalanche.

Such is why growth in the spiritual life is not about us doing something but about our hearts being converted to the *reality* of what God in Christ has already done. The garment of salvation is already ours through Christ. The shoe is already yours. The meaning of life is to grow into that shoe and to *walk* in newness of life (Rom 6:4).

And so as you read, please remember: we don't need to climb out of the darkness. We have a Rescuer who has climbed down and set us on solid ground and turned us around. Jesus our Rescuer longs to give direction to our lives. We need not make a name for ourselves. Our Rescuer has *already* named us and spiritual growth is about learning from Him *who we already are.*

"But by the grace of God," he said, "I was able to remain calm and think." This book is an invitation to do just that.

CHAPTER 1

The Big Why

The more I become an "adult," the more I want to become a child again. I admire a child's questioning nature. My brother-in-law Jamie asked a lot of questions as a child and so his parents placed him on a strict ten question per day limit. When a child first learns to ask the question *why*, it will take years for him to stop asking. "It is time to go to bed. *Why?* Because I said so. Why? Because I'm in charge. Why?"

Of course those are all small *why* questions. Eventually we get to *the big why*. Why are we here? Why did God create us? Why were we made? God wove *the big why* question into our DNA and eventually we all get around to asking it.

I will never forget the first hopeless answer I ever got to *the big why* question. I was in college. We were reading some philosopher that got rich and famous for *his* response to *the big why*. He basically said that the human race was the random result of atoms colliding. Why are we here? According to this particular philosopher, we are here because of a molecular accident. This is no doubt the most hopeless answer to *the big why* question I've ever heard.

It may surprise you to discover that most people throughout history have given an answer with a similar ring of hopelessness.

If you happened to grow up in the ancient Near East around 1200 BCE, just before the Book of Genesis was written, your world would have been incredibly dark and hopeless. Most people believed that many gods existed and that each god was at war with the others. As a kid you no doubt asked your parents why the gods created you in the first place. There isn't a kid in the world that doesn't get to *the big why* eventually. "We were created because the gods were bored." "We were created because the gods were lonely." "We were created because the gods were lazy and needed free labor." In other words, in the ancient Near East there was no *why*.

It was into this horribly dark and hopeless world that these words from Scripture were first recorded. "In the beginning . . . God created the heavens and the earth . . . And God saw that it was *good* . . . God created humankind in his image, in the image of God he created them" (Gen 1:1, 25, 27).

We don't quite understand how radical and foreign these words would have sounded in their original context. We don't feel the scandal such a claim would have evoked from its first hearers. In 1200 BCE no one had ever conceived that the earth was good, that God was good, or that you and I were created in the image of *a* single God. This concept would have been as foreign to that world as the telephone.

What was and is so scandalous about the Biblical worldview is that we are not only made in God's image but that we were also created to bear God's *likeness* (Gen 1:26). Of course, this will make us wonder what exactly God *is like* in the first place, a question this book will answer in due time. However, our familiarity with sayings like "God is good" or "we are infinitely valuable" sometimes leads to overfamiliarity. And the moment *anything* becomes overfamiliar to us, it loses its transformative power. Such is why I want us to feel the controversy, scandal, and shock the Bible would have no doubt been to its first hearers. "You are made in the image of a good God. You are infinitely precious and intended to bear the *likeness* of the goodness that only belongs to God." These words were written to a hopeless world and nothing has ever been the same.

The Bible and "The Big Why"

I increasingly believe that the Bible's answer to *the big why* has the power to transform our life. It says we were created to reveal, reflect, and *image* a very good God as we grow into God's own *likeness*.

In contrast to a warring pantheon, the Bible reveals a supra-personal, loving God. The God of the Bible has three distinct personalities on the one hand, and yet is one. I am referring to the doctrine of the Trinity, which says that the God of the universe is a perfect community of love. The Bible contends that it was *this* Triune God, this Perfect Community, that created both our world and us. As Genesis 1:1 tells us, "God created," which we attribute to the work of the Father. In Genesis 1:2 the *Spirit* of God hovers over the waters, which is the exact same language the gospels use to speak of the Holy Spirit hovering over the water at Jesus' baptism. Finally, Genesis 1:3 tells us that God creates by speaking His *Word*. Creation is not something that God *thinks* into existence. Rather God *speaks*, and creation is called into existence. Christians believe that this "Word" is expressed fully in the person of Jesus Christ.

We all wrestle with *the big why*. We yearn to know what makes life meaningful, as well as what gives us value and significance. How we answer *the big why* often determines whether our life is a blessing or a nightmare.

This is why spiritual growth happens only as we acknowledge that we were not created because God is bored. We were not created because God is lazy. We are not a molecular accident or a cosmic goof. We exist because at the heart of all reality is a wonderful and dynamic Life Christians call the Trinity.

We exist because this God is generous and kind and good, and because God wanted to create us to be what Swiss theologian Karl Barth called "a parable of His own life."[1]

I fear too many of us have forgotten who we are, or like the pre-Genesis ancient Near Easterners were never told in the first place. Many people tend to oscillate between two extremes when it comes to our self-image. One view says we deserve a place equal to God. A few religions even teach that we are divine. On the opposite side of the pole we find the radically scientific and secular viewpoint where humans are a freakish cosmic accident—the random result of a random "bang." Christians accept neither viewpoint. We believe that we are the pinnacles of God's creative work, that we bear the image of the Triune God, and that we are created to share in God's life as we grow into God's likeness.

The Shape of God's Image

Since we exist to be God's image-bearers and to grow into God's likeness, it would be good to put some flesh on what it actually means to live into this purpose. The foundation of growing into our God-given purpose is a clear understanding that we have a dignity and a worth that comes to us from God. "Worthiness" is foundational when we speak of our purpose to grow into God's likeness so that we might "image" God in the world. A belief in our worthiness and goodness and preciousness, apart from what we do or don't do, is central. Christians have a word for the unshakable worthiness we have before God irrespective of what we do or don't do. We call it *grace*. Built on the grace-full foundation of our worthiness before God, the Bible suggests that we reflect God most clearly when we participate in an intimate, life-giving relationship with God and each other, and when we engage in creative, meaningful work.

---

1 Karl Barth's actual phrase is "parable of the existence of his Creator." *Church Dogmatics III.2: The Doctrine of Creation* (New York: T & T Clark International, 2004), 203.

Intimate Relationship

We are created to enjoy an intimate relationship with God and other people. Although we tend to speak of these as separate realities, in truth the two are deeply intertwined. We cannot have an intimate relationship with God and not draw closer to our brothers and sisters. Similarly, we cannot be courageously vulnerable and transparent with other people and not feel a divine tug to draw closer to God.

We were created to converse with God, to delight in God, and to trust in God. The early Church Fathers used the Greek word *parrhesia* to describe the intimacy Adam experienced with God in the Garden of Eden. *Parrhesia* implies a relationship characterized by freedom, boldness, and sincerity. *Parrhesia* is about showing God and others our "secret self." The Book of Genesis infers that Adam and God took an intimate, nightly walk together in the cool of the day. Adam was naked, a symbol for being fully known and comfortable in the presence of God.

I can't imagine that Adam was ashamed to walk naked with God. In fact we can only assume that God was naked as well. To be in the nude must have felt like the most natural thing in the world for Adam. Like an innocent child with the Father he admired so much, Adam walked nightly with his God, his friend, and his hero. Basking in the created world, Adam no doubt asked a million different *big why* questions as he continually explored the magnificence and wonder of life and of his place at the center of God's "very good" created realm.

Adam was exactly what God created him to be. He was wholly whole and fully himself. Adam was a *priest,* for to live was to worship and to worship was to breathe. Life was a natural and glorious exercise in reflecting back to God all of the goodness and love that God so freely poured into him. The word *interpenetration* seems to me the best descriptor of the perfect relationship that God and Adam enjoyed. God lived inside of Adam and Adam lived inside of God.

Intimacy with Others

Human relationships seem much more in our reach of understanding. We intuit at a deep level that to live meaningful lives we
must learn to love other people. Thomas Merton said it's impossible to become fully "us" until we learn to truly love another
person.[2]

The Book of Genesis gives us a wonderful picture of Adam's
life with God before "the fall." There is no sin, no disobedience, and nothing that damages Adam's relationship with God.
Genesis also tells us that everything that God has created thus
far is good. "God created the heavens and the earth, and God
saw that it was *good*." The light was good, the ocean was good,
and the plants were good. The "goodness" of God's created
world is the constant refrain of Genesis in chapter one. It was
all "good," that is until we get to Genesis 2:18.

For the first time God looks at the man and says, "not good!"
Someone once told me God says "not good" because God likes
women better. But I think the reason God says "not good" is
because Adam is "alone." A better translation of the Hebrew
Bible would be that Adam was "disconnected."

Like each and every one of us, God created Adam to connect with other people at a deep, meaningful level. God created
Adam for authentic and transparent relationships. There is only
one problem. There is no one for Adam to connect with!

The Genesis story then takes a dark and comedic twist. God
becomes Adam's wingman. Adam is lonely and God decides to
"set him up." God makes a bunch of animals and parades them
in front of Adam so he can choose a partner to "connect" with
from among them. Adam is all alone in Eden and God brings
to him animal after animal—horse, buffalo, cat, lizard, rat,
cheetah—and God essentially says, "Adam, these are *for you*.

2 Thomas Merton, *Disputed Questions* (Louisville, KY: Trustees of the Merton Legacy Trust,
   1988).

Take your pick!" But as the story goes, "for the man there was not found a helper as his partner" (Gen 2:20). Adam's situation remains the same. Adam is still not connected with another person. *"Not good."*

The Bible then introduces us to Eve. God sends Adam into a deep sleep and forms Eve from Adam's rib. This act is meant to symbolize their deep interconnectedness as well as their common grounding in God, creation, and each other. Adam awakes and screams *at last!* "This at last is bone of my bones and flesh of my flesh!" (Gen 2:23). It is here, for the first time, that we are told that Eden was a nudist colony. "The man and his wife were both naked, and were not ashamed" (Gen 2:25).

I like to imagine Adam's walk with God after seeing Eve for the first time. Was it difficult for Adam to leave her? Did Adam *really* want to walk with God that night, or did he prefer to stay with Eve? I don't really know. What I do know is that Adam felt so loved and so blessed by his God, his friend, and his hero. His God was always surprising him and blessing him with amazing new experiences and gifts.

I imagine Adam and God talked about how beautiful Eve was and about how much fun he was having getting to know her. When I began dating my wife Emily, I'm not sure I talked to God about anything else! It's no coincidence that our first dance as a married couple was to Etta James' *At Last!*[3]

As for Eve, she must have felt so safe, loved, and cherished. She didn't feel used or taken for granted. She knew, in a way that no woman has ever known since, that she was appreciated and admired for who she was. Adam *knew* her because he *saw* her complete, naked, and secret self fully. Life in the nudist colony was good. Eve had a deep and intimate relationship with both Adam and God. That was, after all, why she existed in the first place.

---

3 Actually, Mack Gordon wrote *At Last* in 1941. Etta James renewed the song's popularity when she released a version in 1960.

I worked as a hospital chaplain a couple years ago and I had the privilege of being at the bedside of many dying people. I clearly remember two types of people. I met plenty of people who had measured their success by what they achieved. They had accomplished great things but never really connected with God or even their own family. They had a stockpile of wealth and power and social status, but like Adam before he met Eve, they were disconnected. Each one died with bitter regrets, or with bitter complaints, depending on whether they blamed others or themselves for their "lot" in life.

I also remember a second group, which I will call "connectors." These connectors measured their success by the relationships they formed and nurtured over the course of their lives. They were deeply committed to their family and friends. They had learned well the art of giving and receiving love. Their funerals, I was told, were standing room only. Not one of them regretted having lived their life for their God, their friends, their neighbors, their children, their family, or their church— not a single one.

I had a Bible study leader once that would always say we have a God-shaped hole in our heart that only God can fill. I think he was right. As St. Augustine once said, "our souls are restless until they rest in Thee, O Lord."[4] But a second and less obvious truth exists that we far too often ignore. We all have a human-shaped hole that God chooses not to fill.

I do not mean to suggest that we all need to get married or be romantically involved. However, Adam was with God before "the fall" and according to the Bible he was still disconnected. Adam had a human-shaped hole in his heart. No substitute, including God's Self, could fill that hole.

No substitute can fill our need to connect deeply with other people either. Not money. Not busyness. Not business. Not

---

4 *Confessions of Saint Augustine*, written by Bishop Augustine of Hippo between CE 397 and CE 398.

casual sex. Not casual conversation. Not looks. Not books. Not brains. Not achievement. Not alcohol. Not even our daily private time with God. Adam was in a state of sinless perfection, and yet Genesis tells us that he was "disconnected." According to God, that's "not good."

Creative Work

An intimate, life-giving relationship with God and other people is important but by itself relationship cannot answer *the big why*. Creative, meaningful work also lies at the heart of why we exist.

We hear something radical and shocking in Genesis 2:2: God "finished the work that he had done." The idea that God works was perhaps more shockingly scandalous than the notion that God loves us, especially when we place the Bible alongside other creation accounts of the day. For example, in the "Enuma Elish" we find the Babylonian creation myth with its views on the dignity of human work.[5] The Enuma Elish tells the story of a great battle between the gods. In the ancient Near East, the gods were always at war with one another. A tale is told of the bold and daring young Marduk who wins a great battle of the gods. Marduk celebrates by slashing open the belly of one of the defeated gods. As the story goes, out of that dead, defeated god's belly came the world you and I inhabit.

Marduk is gracious. He invites the other gods to live on the earth and to enjoy its resources. But the gods soon discover that keeping up with the earth is a full-time job! The gods come up with a solution. They create humans to do the work they are too lazy to do.

The Babylonians had an incredibly low view of work. But so did the Greeks. Greek myth tells the story of Pandora's

---

5 Many believe that the Enuma Elish was composed in the Bronze Age (roughly eighteenth to sixteenth centuries BCE). Some scholars favor an earlier date of 1100 BCE. See http://en.wikipedia.org/wiki/Enuma_Elish.

Box. According to legend, Zeus gave a woman named Pandora a beautiful box and said, "Under no circumstances are you to open this!" Unable to curb her curiosity, Pandora did what any seven-year-old would do. She opened the box! And in that box Pandora discovered all the evils and sickness of the world—death, decay, disease, Brussels sprouts, and of course *work!* Like the Babylonians before them, the Greeks had an incredibly low view of human work.

One can begin to see how the Bible was and is so scandalous, unique, and different. The Bible says work has dignity because God works. "In the beginning" God plants a garden. Work is not beneath God. Creative, meaningful work is something that God delights in and created us to experience.

Many Greeks taught that if you *had to work*, the only noble profession was to become a philosopher. Philosophers, after all, don't have to get their hands dirty. In light of all this, it is humbling to consider that Jesus spent thirty years of his life working as a blue-collar carpenter. Jesus had more in common with factory workers than he did with the tenured professor or the priest.

If nothing else, the Bible's high view of work should make us reconsider our picture of "the good life." Paradise is not an extended vacation or about acquiring enough money to relax, eat cake, and do nothing. Paradise is about beauty and friendship and God and *work*. Creative and meaningful work is at the heart of *the big why*. Not to get too far ahead of ourselves, but Christians call the meaningful work God has given us to do "mission." But we will say more about this later.

Of course we need to distinguish between *creative* work and transactional work. Like God we exist to *create*. It is entirely true that the word *create* is only used with respect to God in the Bible. God alone creates *ex nihilo*—"out of nothing." But the Bible does use words like "shape" and "form" to describe our work with God in creation, which is obviously different. God creates out of nothing, whereas we form and shape the "stuff" that God creates *ex nihilo. Like God we exist to bring order out of chaos.*

The Bible portrays God's Spirit hovering over "a formless void" and "the face of the deep" so that the Spirit might bring order out of the mess (Gen 1:2). God then begins to separate things. God separates light from darkness, night from day, and the sky from the ground. God's "work" is to take that which is chaotic and without form so as to impose a new and wonderful design on it. This is what creative, meaningful work is all about—bringing order out of chaos.

There is a reason we love to make things "from scratch" and delight in making "something out of nothing." We exist to bring order out of chaos like God. Whether we are a teacher bringing out the potential of our students, or a musician turning a jumbled set of lyrics and notes into a song, or a landscaper turning an overgrown yard into a garden, or an aspiring author taking his thoughts on Christianity and ordering them into a book, we all delight in a job well done. We love, as my prayer book says, tasks that demand our best efforts and accomplishments that satisfy and delight us.

Now at this point we need to up the ante a bit. It is not enough to say that we were created to work. Our vocation to create goes much deeper than this. We were created as vessels through which God could continue *God's work*. God's great desire is to rule in and through the humans God created. The Bible records God as saying, "Let us make humankind in our image, according to our likeness; and let them have dominion" (Gen 1:26). We are not only priests but also *kings* with a certain amount of "dominion" over God's created world.

Of course we must understand our kingly vocation in light of *how God would rule* the natural world. I know this is hard in a world where the ice caps are melting and the ozone layer continues to thin. Dominion is *not* domination, and the Biblical concept of "dominion" can by no means justify humanity's abuse of the earth. We recall that the human is placed in the garden to "till" God's created world (Gen 2:15). The Hebrew word translated "till" literally means *to serve*. God's "dominion" is tied to service, not exploitation. God created us to serve the world as we take responsibility for engaging in meaningful and creative work.

We were created to *work* with God and for God as representatives on earth. There is a reason we all hunger to "do something that makes a difference." Engaging in creative, difference-making work is also at the heart of Christianity's answer to *the big why*.

Logos

We have not yet captured the fullness of the Bible's answer to *the big why*. For a fuller answer we turn to the opening words from the Gospel According to John.

> In the beginning was the Word, and the Word was with God, and the Word was God. He was in the beginning with God. All things came into being through him, and without him not one thing came into being. (Jn 1:1–3)

The opening words of this gospel are a clear echo of Genesis 1:1. In the beginning was the "logos," a Greek term translated "Word." When John wrote his account of Jesus' life, the nature of the logos was at the heart of *the big why* debate going on at the time.

Our English word *logic* derives from the Greek word logos. The ancient debate at the time St. John's gospel was penned centered on the logos, or the *logic behind our existence*. To discuss the nature of the logos *is* to ask *the big why*. What is the logic, or rationale, behind our existence? This was the question everyone was asking when St. John wrote his gospel.

The answers actually haven't changed much in two thousand years. One ancient group, the Epicureans, denied that any logos existed. Many of them suggested that we imbibe as much pleasure as possible before we die. This perspective is still very much alive in our world. One musician captures the Epicurean worldview well when he sings, "Eat, drink, and be merry, for tomorrow we shall die."[6] Another group, the Stoics, thought about the logos primarily in terms of their moral behavior and the attainment of virtue. They thought *the big why* was about reigning in their cravings and living a virtuous life.

Most accounts of the logos throughout history, and even today, fall into one of these two camps. There is either no meaning and we should all party, or else meaning is something *we attain* by following the Law and by being a really good person. We can run away from home and spend our money on our pleasures, or else we can stay home and follow every rule to the tee (see Lk 15:11–32). Such is the way of the Epicurean and Stoic, whether they are ancients or moderns.

The Christian way is much different. We believe that the logos, or the logic behind our existence, is a person to know, love, embrace, hug, eat with, and experience. We believe Jesus Christ is the Logic behind our lives. Only in Him can we find the intimacy and meaning we were created for. That is why Christianity isn't a philosophy or a set of principles, but a power. St. Paul calls it the "power of God for salvation to everyone who has faith" (Rom 1:16).

All religions answer *the big why* in one way or another. For Muslims it is the Koran. For Buddhists it is the eightfold path. For secular religion it is pleasure. For Christians it is Jesus.

I am not yet trying to persuade you that Jesus Christ is the logos, though I certainly believe that He is in fact the answer to *the big why*. I sincerely hope the pages that follow give a clear account for what rooting our lives in this truth looks like in

---

6 The Dave Matthews Band is the artist. "Tripping Billies" is the song from the album *Crash* (RCA Records, 1996). I believe he is alluding to 1 Corinthians 15:32.

practical terms. But I do wish to persuade you to take a hard look at your life and to consider what you think the logos of your life is.

I believe that it is impossible to live for nothing. I also believe that courage begins when we tell the truth about what we are living for. Have you pondered lately the logic behind *your* existence? Did you randomly happen or were you created? And if you were created, who or what were you created *for?*

These are not easy questions, but I believe they are important ones. Wrestling with *the big why* isn't easy. But it is ultimately far easier than not wrestling with *the question* of what makes life meaningful. I think back to that first group of people I visited in the final hours of their life. Not one of them wrestled with *the big why* and they all died with bitter regrets.

Wrestling with *the big why* takes courage. I define courage as a continual willingness to wrestle with the "logic" behind our existence coupled with an unswerving commitment to align our lives with that which we discover. If you saw someone using twenty-dollar bills as toilet paper, you would gasp. Money has a different logos than *that*. The same would hold true if you saw someone using a flat-screen TV for target practice. We know money's logos. We know a TV's logos. The real question is, *do we know our own?*

Identity

At the heart of *the big why* is the question of identity—*who am I?* I had a seminary professor who once said that the question of identity is the question of difference. Whatever we think gives our lives meaning matters greatly. How we finish the sentence "I am ____" sets the course of our life.

The book of Genesis defines our identity in a way that the rest of the Bible will echo, reiterate, and expand upon. We are the beloved of God. Each person was created to be both God's priest and God's king. We are all endowed with worth and dignity because we have an unshakable *identity* as God's beloved children. Again, Christians call this *grace*. Our identity is unshakable precisely because it comes as a one-way gift. We may grow into the gift and build our life around the gift, *or not*. But grace is one-way love. We are a "somebody" simply because God has spoken our creation and salvation into existence. God creates it *ex nihilo*.

The implication here is that we are not what we do. We are not how we look. We are not our I.Q. We are not our net worth. We are not our mistakes. We are not our successes. We are people whom God created for a deep and intimate relationship with God's Self and each other. We are people who were created to engage in creative and meaningful work, i.e., people with a "mission" if you prefer such language. The Bible does not merely tell us *why* we are here. The Bible also tells us *who we are*. It speaks to us of a secure and firm and grace-full identity rooted in God.

We are the cherished beloved of God and the bearers of God's image. We are priests. We are kings. We are God's beloved.

The "Real World"

I suspect this chapter has made you present to some mixed feelings. After all, the wonderful, carefree nudist colony that Genesis describes is not the world we inhabit. Perhaps it described reality a long, long time ago in a garden far away. But the "real world" is much different.

Author Tom Wright says that we find ourselves haunted by echoes of a Voice that speaks to us about our purpose.[7] I think

---

7 See Wright's *Simply Christian: Why Christianity Makes Sense* (New York: HarperCollins, 2006). He speaks about this Voice in Part I, entitled "Echoes of a Voice."

Wright's right. We know in our bones that God created us to live in an intimate relationship with God and each other and to engage in creative, meaningful work. If the Bible doesn't convince us of this fact, our dreams probably will.

Yet, we cannot escape our experience of the "real world." We no longer live in a garden but in a war zone somewhere east of Eden. Ours is the world of death, conflict, pride, fear, and addiction. But none of this changes the truth that God created each person in God's own image and desires that we reflect God's likeness. God created each of us for intimate relationships and creative, meaningful work—a vocation that finds its deepest fulfillment in God's Son Jesus Christ.

Has God's image been blurred? Has our vocation been distorted? Do we live at the mercy of forces much stronger than us? Yes. *This too we know in our bones.* But no evil in the world will ever rob us of the great truth that we are all "very good."

"In the beginning God created the heavens and the earth and saw that it was *good*. In the beginning was the Logic for Existence and the logos was with God and the logos was God. God created humankind in his image; in the image of God he created them."

Do you feel the controversy and the scandal—the power to heal and transform the human condition? These words were written to a hopeless world desperate to know *the big why* and nothing has ever been the same.

Discussion Questions

1. When do you first recall asking a "big" question about God or about the meaning of life? What was the question, who did you ask, and how satisfied were you with their answer?

2. Do you think there is a difference between being made in God's "image" and growing into God's "likeness"? If so, what do you imagine God is "like"?

3. If Adam and Eve's nakedness is metaphorical language, what does "nakedness" as an ideal spiritual condition represent?

4. Do you believe that intimacy with God will always lead to greater intimacy with others, and vice versa?

5. Like God we were created for meaningful work that brings order out of chaos. Is meaningful work necessarily the same thing as "the job we get paid to do"? What are some examples of "meaningful work" that we don't get paid to do?

6. I define the word *logos* as meaning the "logic for our existence." What does it mean to say that Jesus is the logos?

7. There is a difference between the world we desperately want to live in and the one we currently inhabit. How do you reconcile that in your mind? What has gone wrong? How might the world be put right?

What's Wrong with the World

A newspaper once posed the question, "What's wrong with the world?" The great G. K. Chesterton apparently mailed in this response. "Dear, sirs: I am. Sincerely yours, G. K. Chesterton."[1]

We must all square with the fact that we do not live in God's garden anymore. The world we inhabit is a wreck. But then again so are we. Chesterton was right to acknowledge that the great problem that needs fixing isn't only "out there" but also within each one of us.

The third chapter of Genesis can be hard to stomach. The Bible begins with God, Adam, and Eve enjoying a deep and intimate relationship. There were no secrets between them or lies that separated them. They were both "naked and not ashamed." Every aspect of their body, soul, and psyche was fully on display. Adam and Eve were fully seen, loved, and celebrated. This whole situation, the Bible explains, was "very good."

But then something "happened." Christians have traditionally referred to this happening as "the fall." Although God created humanity for an intimate relationship with Himself and

---

1 Timothy J. Keller, *The Prodigal God: Recovering the Heart of the Christian Faith* (New York: Penguin Group, 2008), 53.

each other and for creative, meaningful work, we "fell" from that reality through our own disobedience.

People debate whether Genesis' account of "the fall" actually happened. It's an interesting question, but I'd like to pose a different one. *Does* it happen? Does Genesis 3 accurately describe our world, and our lives, *right now?*[2]

> **Narrator:** Eve is with her husband in the Garden of Eden. Both are naked as they stand beside the Tree of the Knowledge of Good and Evil. A snake slivers up to Eve and "asks" a question.
>
> **Serpent:** So God actually said you can't eat from *any* of the trees? (Gen 3:1)
>
> **Eve:** No, we can eat fruit from all of the trees *except* this one next to me right in the middle of the garden. In fact, we can't even touch this tree—or we'll die! (Gen 3:2–3)
>
> **Serpent:** That's a bunch of B.Sssssssss. You're not going to die! God only told you that to keep you from being *like* Him. (Gen 3:4–5)
>
> **Narrator:** Eve looks intently at the forbidden fruit and begins to think that it's probably pretty tasty. But the idea of being like God sounds even better! And so after grabbing the fruit and taking a bite she hands the fruit to Adam. Seeing that Eve is still alive, Adam also eats of the fruit. Immediately, both sense that something is different. Adam and Eve begin to examine their bodies in fear. Adam looks at Eve and sees a stranger. Eve looks at Adam and is filled with a horrible sense of shame. They run in opposite directions in an effort to "clothe" themselves with loincloths made from fig

---

2 This creative summary of Genesis 3 is a faithful interpretation.

leaves. They both sit alone and sob. They then hear a sound. Footsteps approach. (Gen 3:6–8)

God: Adam? Adam? Where are you? (Gen 3:9)

Adam: Hiding. When I heard you coming, I got scared and I hid. I'm naked. You can't see me like this. (Gen 3:10)

God: How did you figure out that you were naked? Did you disobey me and eat from the *one tree* that I said was off limits? (Gen 3:11)

Adam: I'm not taking the blame for this! Eve is the one that gave it to me. She took the fruit and ate first! And don't forget *Who it is* that put (the temptress) Eve here in the garden with me in the first place! (Gen 3:12)

God: What do you have to say for yourself, Eve? What have you done? (Gen 3:13a)

Eve: It's the serpent's fault. He tricked me. (Gen 3:13b)

Narrator: God is sad and struggles to make sense of what has happened. He feels betrayed and for the first time God sees something on the earth that is not what He intended. God looks around—"not good." God's heart breaks. In silence, God and his two image-bearers walk slowly to the Gate of Eden. Adam and Eve cover themselves with loincloths they make for themselves. They are ashamed and do not want to be seen as naked and fallen. God knows that in their self-torment they cannot stay in Eden any longer, which causes God great pain. He swears to Himself that He will do whatever it takes to get them back. No words are spoken as God hands Adam and Eve two sets of clothing that He made for them out of animal skins.

God wants to send them out in the clothes He makes for them, not the ones they make for themselves. Adam and Eve leave the Garden. Each one is utterly alone. (Gen 3:20–23)

Does It Happen?

The saga of "the fall" begins with a question. "Did God really say that you cannot eat from any of the trees?" If one reads the Bible carefully, it becomes quickly obvious that God said no such thing. God generously permitted them to eat from *all* of the trees in the garden except for one. The serpent, which the Bible later identifies as the Devil (Rev 12:9), intentionally mis-quotes God. *Why?*

My suspicion is that the serpent's strategy was the same then as it is now. The serpent wants Eve to question whether or not God is really good. Behind every blatant act of disobedience against God is a deeply ingrained belief that God is not good. If God *were good*, if God really had our best interest at heart, He would not forbid the very thing we desire! Or so goes our subconscious "thinking."

It rarely occurs to us that what we desire is poison or that, not being omniscient like God, we simply do not know what is best for us.[3] It is not a coincidence that the forbidden tree was named "the Tree of the *Knowledge* of Good and Evil" (Gen 2:17). We all know what's good and evil *for ourselves*. We don't need God to tell us. At least, that's how most of my life is lived.

Eve's response to the serpent is also quite telling. "No, we can eat from all the trees except this one," she says. "In fact, we can't even touch this tree. If we touch it, we will die." This of course is a blatant lie. God never told Adam and Eve that

---

3 The word *omniscient* means all-knowing. An omniscient being has unlimited knowledge of everything. It is an attribute that belongs only to God.

touching the Tree of Knowledge was off limits or that they would die if they touched it. Adam and Eve are trying to convince themselves that God is much harsher than He actually is. If Adam and Eve can convince themselves that God is unreasonable and severe, then disobeying Him won't be as difficult. It is a lot easier to divorce your spouse when you have convinced yourself that she is a hate-filled, controlling jerk. In the same way, when we think that God is an unreasonable megalomaniac or some out-of-touch tyrant, "we'd be crazy" not to bend the rules here and there.

Adam and Eve's eyes are now opened and what a nightmare they see. The beauty that permeated every aspect of life in God's garden is gone. Adam and Eve are now alienated from themselves, from each other, from God, and from the meaningful work God created them to enjoy. Before "the fall" Adam was accustomed to a nightly walk with God in the garden. Now he feels compelled to hide. Adam and Eve are isolated and alone. Their lives have closed in upon them. They are both utterly ashamed.

The Dark Prison

The entire assumption behind a book about growing into Christian maturity is that, at present, we are *not* spiritually mature and that, without a sufficient kind of understanding, will not become spiritually mature people. There is something that hinders us. A great roadblock stands in our way. That roadblock is *shame,* which is a deep sense that we are unworthy to stand naked before God and each other and to live in God's garden.

Genesis notes a fundamental change in Adam and Eve's psyche that occurs directly after their disobedience. The man and woman, who have known nothing but mutuality and intimacy, now look at themselves and each other and are filled with a deep sense of shame. As Genesis recounts, "The eyes of both were opened, and they *knew that they were naked*; and they sewed fig leaves together and made loincloths for themselves" (Gen 3:7, italics mine). Shame is a natural response to feeling the truth of our pitiful condition east of God's perfect garden. We feel unworthy and as a result desperately try to cover ourselves up.

Shame is the legacy of the fall, and it permeates every aspect of our wrecked world and our wrecked lives. Shame is something we all have but few of us are willing to talk about. It's impolite to talk about shame. But talk about it we must to understand the Christian Gospel. Shame is the dark prison that controls our lives. As one researcher defines it, "Shame is the intensely painful feeling or experience of believing that we are flawed and therefore unworthy of love and belonging."[4] Shame is *not* the same thing as guilt. Guilt says, "I did something bad." Shame, on the other hand, is about our *identity*. Shame says, "I am bad."

An Attack on our Identity

In the previous chapter we saw that as soon as we begin exploring *the big why* we eventually come to the question of identity. We are all desperate for an identity. We must know what *our logos,* or the logic behind *our* existence, is. It is impossible to talk about becoming spiritually mature unless we wrestle with the question of whom or what "gives" us an identity, and how shame plays a role in our search.

I truly believe that our world, and far too many of our churches, are seriously confused about what motivates human beings and about how people become spiritually mature. Contrary to what many believe, God did not invent shame to keep us

---

4 Brené Brown, *The Gifts of Imperfection: Let Go of Who You Think You're Supposed to Be and Embrace Who You Are* (Center City, MN: Hazelden, 2010), 39.

in line. Shame is the fruit of the fall. It has no part in God's "very good" creation. Shame is the problem and not part of the solution.

Shame, Isolation, and the False Self

One of the first things we see after the fall is that shame and isolation, unworthiness and aloneness, and hiding and selfishness cannot be separated. Shame, self-alienation, and isolation go hand in hand precisely because the trademark of shame is an accusing, tormenting self-consciousness. As John Bradshaw explains, "To feel shame is to feel seen in an exposed and diminished way."[5] As a result of this painful experience of shame, we forge a self that is "false." It is a self that is false in the same sense that the loincloths Adam and Eve made for themselves were false. They were "false" because they were a desperate attempt to cover their selves and not be exposed as naked and fallen.

Growing up spiritually requires that we understand a pretty basic truth about the human condition. *We all have our loincloths.* We all forge a false self in a desperate attempt to cover up our "nakedness." We all manufacture our own logos. We all construct our own identity apart from God.

I do not believe one can become a mature Christian without a ruthless assessment of what his loincloths are. Apart from an honest acknowledgment of the many and varied ways that we cover ourselves up to make ourselves feel like our life has meaning and importance, we are doomed to a life of immaturity. "As the false self is formed, the authentic self goes into hiding. Years later the layers of defense and pretense are so intense that one loses all awareness of *who one really is*."[6] The

---

5 John Bradshaw, *Healing the Shame That Binds You* (Deerfield Beach, FL.: Health Communications, Inc., 1988), 13.
6 Ibid., 14, italics mine.

question of identity is the question of difference. We cannot speak of who we are until we assess and acknowledge what we are not—the false self comprised of the loincloths we have used to construct an identity so that others don't see us as naked and fallen and unworthy.

At a deep, deep level, we all sense how shabby our loincloths are. The "self" we portray to the world is just that—a portrait. I don't believe that our gifts and vocations are irrelevant or that our lives are a complete mirage. But the emotional labor that comes with polishing our false self is high.

We are so deeply afraid of showing others who we are. When God begins questioning Adam's whereabouts, Adam responds, "I hid *because I was afraid.*" And so rather than show other people our faults, we point out and blame others for theirs. Though Adam and Eve bear mutual responsibility for their sin, they seek to justify themselves as individuals. Adam blames both God and Eve. Eve blames the snake. Too ashamed to face what they have done, Adam and Eve do not take responsibility for their actions. *And that does happen.* Blaming God, the world, and other people is so much easier than taking responsibility for one's life.

I use the term "loincloths" as a metaphor for the ways we "dress up" like Adam and Eve to convince the world that we're "okay" and worthy. Our loincloths are the false self we have constructed to "get by" East of Eden. And at the end of the day, it matters little how fancy and wonderful our loincloths are, or how many people "buy what we're selling." Each one of us senses at a deep, deep level that we are completely and utterly alone. This cosmic alienation resides deep in our subconscious and manifests itself in anger, depression, shyness, or perhaps passive aggressive behavior. Many of us don't know how truly alone we are. Such is the depth of our denial and delusion. But there is no beating the system. A "false self" can never be anything but *false*. There is an incredible sense of loneliness that comes with living a lie.

Sin

The word that we have not yet used is sin. Sin is such a loaded and misunderstood word in today's world that more often than not it is unhelpful. Let me offer my working definition of sin.

Sin is the fruit of a shame-filled life. It is an addictive and destructive spiral of replacing God with "loincloths" of our own making.

This is not how most of us "learned sin." Whether schooled by a well-intentioned parent or Sunday school teacher, or perhaps by a Christian wagging his finger at the way we patterned our lives, we have probably come to understand sin as "disobeying God's commands." In this mental model of sin, God has a list of rules. Some of these rules we understand and some of these rules we do not. But sin, we believe, is what happens when we break those rules.

I'm not saying it's entirely wrong to define sin as rule-breaking. I just think it is incomplete. It is like referring to a dog as an animal, or saying that a banana is best understood as a piece of fruit. Both statements are true, but also incomplete and misleading.

Sin, Shame, and Addiction

I find it most helpful to think of sin as our constant and compulsive attempt to cover ourselves up. In a shame-filled world, this comes as naturally to us as breathing.

Shame is the painful awareness that we experience life as a cracked and divided self. When we lack an inner sense of worthiness, we must search for that sense of worth on the outside.

Born exiled, we do not possess an unshakable inner sense of our worthiness. The result is that we "steal" our sense of worth from the outside—from our job, our looks, our achievements, our relationships, our performance, our sense of humor, or from some other outside source. We are looking for worth where it cannot be found—that's the problem. Yes, some of us find our worth for a season in life. We get the girl. We get the bonus. We get the recognition. We dance our dance and get the world to clap and whistle. But it never does seem to last (does it?) and we are left once again with the painful void.

This is our dilemma. We desperately need to know that our lives have worth, and yet not one of us knows that our life has worth. What's wrong with the world? *Dear Sirs, I am.*

Our Need for Worth

Our search for self-worth is *the* condition of our life. Exiled from God's garden, we seek a sense of worth, or for an identity, where it cannot be found—outside of Eden, and apart from the God who created us in the first place. We are like people trying to light a match under water. We can try as hard as we want but it just won't work. Stealing worth is all we've ever known and so we get our fixes wherever we can. Our lives easily become fruitless and addictive searches for living water in the midst of empty wells. As John Bradshaw puts it:

> The cycle begins with the false belief system that all addicts have, that no one could want them or love them as they are. In fact, addicts can't love themselves. They are an object of scorn to themselves. This deep internalized shame gives rise to distorted thinking. The distorted thinking can be reduced to the belief that I'll be okay if I drink, eat, have sex, get more money, work harder, etc. The shame turns one into

what Kellogg has termed a "human doing," rather than a human being. *Worth is measured on the outside, never on the inside.*[7]

It is good to remind ourselves that Genesis was not written for Adam and Eve.

The Bible was written for us. Genesis is about us. *We* are exiled from the garden. *We* lack an unshakable identity in this world. *We* are haunted and hunted by the monsters of alienation, fear, and blame. *We* are stuck on an addictive treadmill of trying to find loincloths to cover our nakedness, hoping against hope that they will convince the world, and ourselves, that we are "worth" something.

Recovering Sin

It is absolutely vital that we recover a language around sin that is hopeful, accurate, and true to the human experience. The Church has not been a huge help. Most liberals ignore sin. If they speak of sin at all, they usually reduce sin to unjust social structures, or speak of sin as the polar opposite of "inclusion." Right-wingers speak of sin a little too loudly and at times far too contemptuously. God, they assure us, is pretty pissed off at how we're living our lives and so we better shape up.

The best definition of sin I have ever come across comes from Søren Kierkegaard. "Sin is the despairing refusal," he said, "to find your deepest identity in your relationship and service to God. Sin is seeking to become oneself, to get an identity, apart from Him."[8]

---

7 Ibid., 16–17, italics mine.
8 This quote is taken from Kierkegaard's 1849 book, *The Sickness Unto Death: A Christian Psychological Exposition for Upbuilding and Awakening.* However, I first encountered it in Dr. Timothy Keller's *The Reason for God: Belief in an Age of Skepticism* (New York: Dutton, 2008).

His point is that sin is more about filling voids than breaking laws. The broken laws are only a *symptom*. The underlying cause is that we're desperate to forge an identity for ourselves with loincloths of our own making. What all this means is that at the heart of sin is a wrecked relationship—with God, with our selves, with each other, and with the work God created us to delight in. Sin is par for the course when you live east of Eden. *It just happens.*

We are all born with a desperate need for significance and self-worth. We all need an identity—something that makes "us" *us*. The problem is that whatever we build our life around can easily become our god. Sin, therefore, is what happens when we draw an identity from something or someone other than God, which always results in *addiction*. This is a "substitution" we all make. Apart from Christ, this is not a mistake we can avoid. But it is something we can understand.

Spiritual Attraction

Sin has to do with what attracts our hearts. No one constructs their identity from something that repulses them. A woman born into an upper-class family on the East Coast will not construct an identity by becoming a white supremacist. White supremacy simply will not attract her heart and make her feel like "a somebody." But a young man born into a family of neo-Nazis who feels limited in his options very well might "sin" in that particular way. Sin begins when our heart covets something or someone. The reason Adam and Eve ate the fruit was because it "was a delight to the eyes" from a tree that "was to be desired" (Gen 3:6).

This is why the Bible's primary metaphor for sin is not a legal metaphor but a sexual one. The books of Hosea and Jeremiah give us wonderful examples. God is portrayed as a Bridegroom and God's people are depicted as the adulterous wife that chases after lovers they find more attractive than God. The Biblical view of sin has less to do with breaking God's rules than it does with breaking God's heart. We replace God with loincloths of our own making ("idols" to use the Bible's language), and because God's heart is pure and soft and vulnerable and not at all stony like ours, the heart of God breaks—just like it did when Adam and Eve had to leave Eden.

Whenever we sin, there is an attraction happening at the spiritual level infinitely more potent than anything we are capable of feeling at the sexual level. We speak a lot in our world about our "sex drive." The Bible often alludes to our "spirit drive." The problem from the Bible's perspective is that our spirits are driven to adore the wrong things.

Sin and "Religion"

The Puritans called our "spirit drives" our "affections." Our affections have to do with what we are attached to and most fond of in the deep recesses of our heart. The word *religion* derives from the Latin *ligare*, which means to "bind or connect." Our "religion," therefore, is tied to our affections. Whatever we bind or connect our hearts to is our functional religion. Sin is binding or connecting our heart to something or someone other than God.

We see a wonderful example of this in Jesus' encounter with a woman of Samaria in the Gospel According to John.[9]

> **Narrator:** Jesus sits alone by a well in the heat of the day. A woman of Samaria approaches.
>
> **Jesus:** Give me a drink of water from the well.
>
> **Woman:** Jews hate Samaritans and rarely speak to them. Why are you talking to *me?*

---

9 This is my interpretation of John 4:7–18. It is faithful to the Biblical text.

Jesus: If you knew God's gift, and who it is that you are speaking with, you would ask *me* for living water and I would give it to you.

Woman: That's silly. You don't have a bucket and it's a very deep well. Where would you even get your "living water"?

Jesus: Everyone who drinks water from this well will need to keep coming back. What I am offering you is water that will assuage your thirst forever. You will never be thirsty again if you drink my water.

Woman: Then give it to me! I'm sick of walking to this well every day!

Jesus: Go call your husband and come back.

Woman: Don't have one.

Jesus: No you don't. You've had *five husbands,* and right now you're living with a man who won't even marry you.

It always used to bother me that Jesus asked this poor woman about a husband that he was well aware she did not have. It felt like he was rubbing her face in the dirt. *Was Jesus trying to shame her for making so many poor choices?* But then one day it clicked. When Jesus tells this woman to go fetch her husband, Jesus is not being mean. He's trying to nudge her towards a greater level of awareness.

Jesus loves this woman and would never try and shame her. Jesus understands that shame is the fruit of the fall and was never a part of God's "very good" creation. What Jesus *does* do is ask this woman to look at her loincloths. He holds up a mirror. Jesus' intention is to show this woman where she keeps dropping the bucket of her heart to steal a sense of worth from the outside.

Jesus wants her to come to terms with how fruitless and unsuccessful her search for worth has been. Jesus wants this woman to see her functional religion, her "spirit drive," and what her heart has always tried to steal worth from. In her case it was "men."

Sin is the fruit of a shame-filled life. It is the addictive and destructive spiral of replacing God with some other "loincloth" of our own making. To this woman Jesus said, "Go and get your husband!" I wonder what Jesus would say to us.

> **Me:** Give it to me! I want the living water!

> **Jesus:** Go and get your career. Go and get your family. Go and get your need to be liked. Go and get your desperate need to control things. Go and get your need to be appreciated and your obsession with appearance and knowledge and fame and being viewed as a success. Go and get your need for more friends and more money and more status and more respect. Go and get *YOUR* loincloths and put them right next to me! Because I came to give you a new garment that will never wear out. No one will ever assuage your deep spiritual thirst like I can.

Jesus understands our predicament in life outside the garden. We all long for meaning, worth, and security; and yet, regardless of how hard we try, we cannot manufacture or steal worth for ourselves. God wants nothing more than to restore to us that which has been lost. As God says in Psalm 12:5, "I will place them in the safety for which they long."

The question in the spiritual life is not whether or not we long for safety, meaning, worth, and security, or for what I call an identity. We build our life around finding these things. The question in the spiritual life is always, "What other than God are we tempted to make our primary refuge?" There is always *something* that threatens to attract our heart more than God.

How Spiritual Attraction Works

There is a reliable pattern at work behind our shame-filled search for meaning in things other than God. This pattern can be summarized in three words: *promotion, addiction, and abandonment.*

Promotion

Spiritual attraction begins when we take a good thing and inflate it in our minds and hearts. We take a person or a job or money and we "pump it up." Promotion happens when we take a good thing and make it an "ultimate thing"—something we deem worthy of binding or connecting our heart to because we think it can provide the safety and significance that we long for.

We often fail to realize that the thing we are promoting is *good* in and of itself. Money is not evil. The love of money, however, *is evil* (1 Tim 6:10). In a similar manner, God gives us our family as a great and wonderful gift. But if we love our father, mother, son, or daughter *more than* Jesus, we cannot be his disciple (Mt 10:37). Serving others is also good. But if our sense of self is tied to our service and if we love to serve others more than we love sitting at Jesus' feet, we are "promoting" service above God (see Luke 10:38–42).

It is not possible to ever love anything *too much*. We cannot love our money too much, or our family too much, or our job too much. We can only love these things *too much in proportion to our love for God*. Sin begins when we promote something in our minds so high that it becomes more attractive to us than God. This whole process usually happens without us being aware of it.

Addiction

Any good Starbucks junkie understands stage two. We get addicted to what we have promoted. We need more and more and more of whatever "substance" we are stealing worth from in order to secure the same "high." This is the law of diminishing returns. A small cup of coffee from time to time used to be just fine. Now four Venti red-eyes a day are necessary to do the trick.[10] It used to make us feel good when our father praised us, but now we base our lives, and sometimes even choose our career, around receiving his praise. It used to make us feel special when others noticed us. But now our happiness depends on taking the center stage.

Again, this is an unconscious process, which is why it is often so deadly. Like my friend Jim says, "We don't know what we don't know" about ourselves. After all, no one gets up every morning and says, "Today I think I'll do the same stupid things I've been doing for decades," and yet inevitably we do. We can no more kick our cynicism or passivism or optimism or racism or materialism or our need to please others than an alcoholic can kick her alcoholism. *We are all caught in the exact same spiral of addiction.* There *really* is not that much of a difference between any of us at all. We are all something-aholics. That is why "12-step" spirituality, rooted in the AA program, is taking on more and more prominence in many churches. Every last one of us is addicted to something. We don't need to try harder. We need an intervention from the outside.

I don't mean to say that all addictions are equal. I would far rather be addicted to jogging than cigarettes. However, I do believe that the same destructive cycle can be at work in both cases and that we should question the cultural consensus that one addiction is "virtuous" while the other is "sinful." All sin involves spiritual attraction and spiritual addiction. The Pharisees and the tax collectors were both prisoners of the exact same cycle. The former were addicted to their own righteousness, the latter to their wallets.

---

10 I heard a rumor that Venti is no longer the largest size Starbucks offers and that it has been replaced with the "Trenta." Come soon, Lord Jesus.

Thankfully, there is always a crisis or breakdown when whatever we promote, steal worth from, and become addicted to fails to make *good on its promise.* Our false gods always let us down. They always abandon us. Nothing is more painful. Yet nothing is more necessary for us to understand and delight in the Christian Gospel.

Abandonment

Whatever we promote above God for our sense of meaning and self-worth will eventually let us down. The "ideal job" becomes a frantic rat race. We discover that the girl we fell in love with has bad breath and weird idiosyncrasies and an agenda not confined to meeting our every need. Our sister has a baby and we sulk because no one pays attention to *us* anymore. We discover that we're not as faithful in prayer as we thought we were (and in this case we derived our sense of self not from God but *from a feeling of self-assurance* that *we* were in fact a "faithful" Christian). Our gods abandon us and the result is always the same. We feel hollow, depressed, anxious, and angry.

Jesus told a story about an arrogant young man that asked his father for his inheritance early. This would be an odd request in today's world, but it was even odder in Jesus' day. The story is traditionally called "The Prodigal Son." In Jesus' story the father honors his son's request and the son squanders his newfound fortune on "dissolute living" (Lk 15:13). The beginning of this story is quite sad because we have to watch as the prodigal son's god, pleasure, abandons him. The son is left starving in a land plagued by famine and he even starts to envy the pigs. He decides to get a job babysitting the pigs because unlike him *they have food.* It is embarrassing. But at the same time, *it happens.*

I see in this story the script we are all living in some capacity. We build our life around someone or something that makes great promises to "save us" from our meaninglessness or boredom or insecurity, and *that something* or *that someone* then becomes our "functional" religion or god. Never does this work out well. As C. S. Lewis explains:

> The longings which arise in us when we first fall in love, or first think of some foreign country, or first take up some subject that excites us, are longings which no marriage, no travel, no learning, can really satisfy. I am not now speaking of what would ordinarily be called unsuccessful marriages, or holidays, or learned careers. I am speaking of the best possible ones. There was something we grasped at, in that first moment of longing, which just fades away in reality.[11]

Our gods always fade away. They never last. We either fail our god—we let down our spouse, we lose our job, or we gain weight. Or more often than not the god we grasp at *fails us*. They do not place us in the safety for which we long. We are left in the pigsty envying the fortune of others.

Perhaps this rings truer as we get older. A "midlife crisis" is nothing more than one big, fat recognition that all the good things we have built our life around are fading away—our youth, our kids, our bodies, our spouse's body, the thrill of climbing the corporate ladder. The gods we have worshipped for decades all leave us and the loincloths we have worn for years now seem as nothing in our eyes.

The Decision

When our loincloths fall off and our gods jump ship and we find ourselves alone, we only have two options. We can continue

---

11 C. S. Lewis, *Mere Christianity* (San Francisco: HarperSanFrancisco, 1952), 135.

worshipping idols and bind our hearts yet again to some "god" we hope can deliver the goods. Or, we can *reorient our lives*. The latter option is repentance.

We all walk the way of option one. No one is exempt, which is why sin is such an addictive and destructive spiral. We see this clearly in the woman of Samaria that Jesus encounters at the well. Her first husband left her. The result was a deep sense of shame and alienation. Her response was to find another husband. Maybe this "god," she thought, wouldn't leave her. But her second husband left as well. The shame and alienation kept building and so she scampered off to find herself a third husband. "This time it will work out," she told herself. "*He* will treat me right. *This one* will make me feel safe." By the time she meets Jesus, she is on her sixth "life partner." She is so shame-filled and alone at this point in her life that the guy she's with won't even marry her.

Alcoholics know how this works. Their drinking intensifies their depression and so in order to numb their depression they make a stronger drink. As one character in an *Austin Powers* movie put it, "I eat because I'm unhappy and I'm unhappy because I eat. It's a vicious cycle." Whether we see it or not, this cycle is at work in all of our lives. In order to ease the pain caused by our own idiotic prescriptions, we self-medicate. We need a more qualified Physician than ourselves—an intervention from the *outside*. This brings us to option two.

We *can* put our ultimate faith in a Lord who will not forsake us, or abandon us when we forsake Him. He can give us "new clothes" to replace our shabby loincloths. We can ask Jesus to help us order our loves rightly under His lordship and leadership, so that we learn the art of loving our family and job and money and body and power and intellect and popularity without worshipping them or asking them to save us. We can repent. Turning from our false gods and reexamining our life's goals and direction and life principles under Jesus' lordship is always an option.

And at the end of the day, this is all that Christianity offers. Not that it is a small thing. But Christianity is not a complex religion. There is One, Christianity teaches, worth binding and connecting our hearts to—Jesus Christ. As Dr. Timothy Keller explains, "Jesus is the only Lord who, if you receive him, will fulfill you completely, and, if you fail him, will forgive you eternally."[12]

Sin and Hope

The Christian Gospel is ultimately about hope. But authentic hope requires a truthful assessment of our condition. We must tell the truth about our lives. We must see how *we* are caught up in the spiral of sin and shame. *Then* we can hope. Such is why for at least two reasons it is a hopeful thing to define sin more as an addictive process of "covering up" (in loincloths or the "false self") than as "breaking the rules."

We are powerless to change ourselves. That's the first good news of sin. At first glance this may seem like horrible news. Trust me when I say that it is not. We live in a world that wants us to pull ourselves up by own bootstraps. The problem is that it's impossible. We do not have the "inner resources" to take away our own loneliness and fear and anxiety, nor can we break our own addictive patterns for any sustained period of time. I credit the success of Alcoholics Anonymous to the wisdom of their twelve steps, the first being, "We admitted we were powerless over alcohol—that our lives had become unmanageable." It takes an arrogant, blind, and foolish man to say that an alcoholic may be powerless over *his addiction* but that we can kick our desperate need to please others or watch pornography or correct others anytime we choose. Reality check: *Our lives have become unmanageable, too.*

---

12 Keller, *The Reason for God*, 173.

Psychologists marvel that we live in a culture where just about everyone lacks self-esteem. This phenomenon is no doubt connected to our societal charade where we berate everyone for not taking control of his or her life when in reality not one of us can do it. The Samaritan woman did not "take control of her life." She met Jesus Christ by a well.

Second, the good news of sin is that our chief identity before God is not best understood as that of *a worthless sinner.* Sin is an addictive and destructive shame-filled spiral of replacing God with something else. The noun in that last sentence was "spiral." I am not a spiral. I am caught in one.

We all sin. No one is exempt. It is also true that we are all so enmeshed in this addictive and destructive spiral of replacing God with other things that it can be a good thing to metaphorically beat our breast and pray, "Have mercy on me, a sinner," or perhaps to acknowledge our status as the "chief" sinner.[13] However, this is a *form* of repentance that is only meant for a "season." Ecclesiastes refers to it as "a time to break down." (Eccl 3:3). However, breast-beating, breaking-down repentance is not an end in itself. It is a sometimes-necessary means to recovering our *true identity* in God.

I am not downplaying the horrid reality of human sin. My intention is to make us *more aware* of sin's presence in our world and our lives. But that does not mean that we should tie sin to *our identity.* Even the most lost among us bears the stamp of God's image, cracked and broken as that image may be. But at *the deepest level,* their identity simply is not tied to what they do or to a vicious sin-cycle they are caught up in.

I see two types of people in the New Testament. I see cracked and broken image-bearers living in a pigsty. The Good Shepherd is seeking them out and inviting them home, and they either have not heard God's invitation or they have not accepted

---

13 See Lk 18:13 and 1 Tim 1:16, respectively.

it. Second, I see cracked and broken image-bearers who have been reborn and given new clothes to replace their shabby loin-cloths. And it can be *very hard* to tell the difference between the two at first glance.

We must define sin in a way that is consistent with Scripture and furthers God's work of removing the roadblock of human shame—not in a way that reinforces shame. Again, there is a difference between "I am bad" and "I did something bad." The truth that we are lost must not negate the much greater truth that we are incredibly valuable to God.

New Clothes

I know the addictive and destructive spiral of sin has its way with all of us. Our lives are a chaotic mess. Our cheese, as Brennan Manning once joked, is falling off our cracker and our halos are all tilted. But as we established in chapter 1, God's "work" is to take that which is chaotic and without form so as to impose a new and wonderful design on it. The God of the Bible brings order out of chaos. This includes the chaos of our lives. It is what the spiritual journey is all about. This journey will no doubt lead us to more intimate relationships with God, each other, and to a new sense of what it means to engage in "meaningful work."

For a story as tragic as "the fall," I find it remarkable that the ending is so chockfull of hope. As the author of Genesis explains, "the Lord God made garments of skins for the man and for his wife, *and clothed them*" (Gen 3:21, italics mine). Immediately after Adam and Eve's catastrophic mistake, God provides them clothes of *His making* to replace their shabby loincloths.

It is significant that the clothes God provides were made from the skins of an animal. The author's point is that for God to provide Adam and Eve with new clothes after "the fall," a sacrifice had to be made. We will look at this theme in the next chapter. But suffice it to say for now that in the Bible shame is never removed without someone making a sacrifice.

I think back on Chesterton's response to that newspaper's question and marvel because his answer is both true on the one hand, but not true on the other. Sin and shame are what is wrong with our world, but the cycle of sin and shame are at work within *my heart,* and that makes *me* wrong with the world, too.

Nevertheless, the Christian Gospel is not as concerned with the question of what is wrong with the world as it is with the question of "How have things been put right?" To put it a bit differently, Christianity's chief concern is not with the Tree of Knowledge but with a much different tree that a Jewish rabbi named Jesus was nailed to nearly two thousand years ago.

And so let us not be concerned any longer with *why* we wear loincloths. A sacrifice has been made. The Father is ready to dress us. A "welcome home" mat has been placed at Eden's door. Our focus must now shift to the new clothes that Jesus provides.

Discussion Questions

1. How do you understand the classic Christian doctrine of "the fall?" Do you imagine it *actually happened?* In what sense does it *still* happen?

2. This chapter asserts that behind every blatant act of disobedience against God is a deeply ingrained belief that God is not good. Do you agree? When are you most tempted to doubt God's goodness?

3. Our experience with shame leads to the creation of a "false self." How does your "false self" manifest itself in the world? In other words, what loincloths do *you* cover yourself in on a routine basis?

4. What does the word "sin" mean to you? Do you think sin has more to do with breaking God's laws or breaking God's heart?

5. Do you think we can "change" ourselves? Why or why not?

6. The first step of Alcoholics Anonymous has to do with admitting our lives are unmanageable. Is this true for *all people,* or just some?

CHAPTER 3

Not Guilty

When I was in college I went to the courthouse to witness one of the final days of a high-profile criminal trial. A young man named John was being tried for murder. Eventually the trial ended, a verdict was reached, and the defendant was asked to rise. I imagine what followed went something like this.

"Ladies and gentlemen of the jury have you reached a verdict?" "We have," replied the foreman. "On murder in the first degree, how do you find?" "*Guilty.*"

I imagine upon hearing the verdict, John was speechless, emotionless, and that he appeared lifeless. For some reason the image of a shackled, lifeless, and guilty John still haunts me to this day. I imagine John being escorted in chains to a cell to wait for sentencing, which in the state of Texas is usually death by lethal injection. The jury had reached a verdict. *Guilty.*

Somewhere along the line John's life had gone wrong. Perhaps he was mentally ill or had an absent father. Maybe he just fell in with the wrong crowd. He definitely made poor choices and I doubt John ever had much luck. But of course the court was not concerned with any of these details. The fact is John *was* guilty and justice demanded that John pay for his crimes.

Obviously John was not this man's real name. John is my name, but we just as easily could have used your name. Something has gone seriously wrong in all of our lives. The addictive and destructive spiral of replacing God with "loincloths" of our own making has all of us in chains. We are addicted to our unwise choices. We get hurt and we choose to hurt back. The problem with the world is not John and "people like him." What is the problem? "Dear, sirs: *I am.*"

Now some might say I am being dramatic and in some sense I suppose I am. After all, "John *killed someone!*" You might object. "I would never do something like that!" But can any of us say that for certain? If you were born into John's family and had John's upbringing and John's social circle and John's intelligence, can you say for *certain* that you would not kill? And should we answer "no," we must then ask, "why not?" What makes us any better than John? I suspect what distinguishes us from John is our family, upbringing, social circle, and intelligence—all things that chose us long before we could ever choose them.

Murderers

Jesus once inferred that we all have murder in our hearts (Mt 5:21–22). This teaching was just as offensive in Jesus' day as it is in ours. And deep down I suspect we would admit that Jesus is absolutely right. We sense at a deep level that God created us for so much more than simply not murdering people. If simply "not murdering" were all it took to please God, the vast majority of us would, well, "not be wrong with the world." But our hearts whisper to us that in fact we're not fine at all. There's a *big why* that goes beyond avoiding murder. God created us for intimacy and meaning, not for keeping our hands off a trigger.

If we are being honest, we *do* murder each other all the time. We kill with our anger, insults, contempt, and indifference. We murder one another with hate-filled words and hate-filled thoughts, with poisonous gossip and character-effacing lies. That doesn't mean we all yell or scream or pitch fits or lose our temper. Many of us have far too much "class" for that. We find it more dignified to kill with our silence, our indifference, and our coldness of heart. Sometimes the best war tactic is to withdraw our support, our encouragement, our generosity, and our favor to prove a point or to get our way. Ignoring others is the best weapon many of us have in our arsenal.

I am not sure if God cares whether we kill one another quickly or slowly, whether we kill someone's body or their spirit, or whether our weapon is a gun or our tongue. *What matters* to God is that we are all in the same boat. Not one of us can take our place on the judge's bench. Indeed Christianity's grounding premise is that we are *all* in need of the mercy of the Court. We are all on trial for murder and we know in our bones the verdict is unfavorable.

It is this inner sense of being condemned, our "inner foreman" so to speak, which contributes so heavily to our shame. We sense at a deep level that we are guilty and therefore not worthy of an intimate relationship with God or even another person. I believe our feelings of unworthiness speak to us of something that is true at the cosmic level. After all, Genesis 3 is *our* story. We are naked outside of Eden trying desperately to cover ourselves with any loincloth we imagine can make us feel worthy again. *The* question of our life then becomes, "From whence is my worthiness to come?"

Worthiness

It is impossible to overemphasize how important *belief in our worthiness* is if we are to experience intimacy with God and one another. The word *worthiness* means "possessing great merit." Unless we believe that we possess the necessary merit to confidently and freely approach God, we will spend our life hiding from God and each other like Adam and Eve did. One either believes that she can stand naked before God and not feel shame, or she doesn't. A person either feels worthy or he doesn't. Belief in our worthiness is critical.

Brené Brown is a shame researcher and has written a wonderful book called *The Gifts of Imperfection*. Brown writes, "If we want to fully experience love and belonging, we must believe we are *worthy* of love and belonging."[1] She then goes on to say something that I think is true, but theologically incomplete. "Our sense of worthiness—that critically important piece that gives us access to love and belonging—lives inside our story."[2] By using the word "story," I assume Brown means the story of our lives. But here's where her words leave me questioning. What if the story of our life is one of constant defeat and reoccurring mistakes and mounting shame? What hope is there for John the murderer? What is so powerful *inside* of John's story that it can erase his every mistake, scrub away his shame, give him the resources to change, and help him know for the first time in his entire life that he is completely worthy of love and belonging? I fear the answer is *absolutely nothing*.

I love Brown's books and would recommend them to all. What she says about the human condition is so true and her writing has helped me immensely. But the question *from whence is our worthiness to come* is a question that transgresses the bounds of science and can only be answered by faith.[3]

Righteousness and the Nature of Forgiveness

The good news of the Christian Gospel is that our worthiness is given to us as a gift from *outside* of our story. The road to healing

---

1 Brown, *The Gifts of Imperfection*, 23.
2 Ibid., 23.
3 Indeed Brown infers as much in *The Gifts of Imperfection*. She notes a 100 percent correlation between being shame resilient and having faith in something Bigger. My hope in this book is to speak to the Christian Gospel's unique perspective on the remedy to human shame.

and joy does not begin with a decision to disregard our shame. On the contrary, healing begins with the honest acknowledgment that, at present, we *are* small, unworthy, and flawed. The Biblical word for the deeply flawed state of our heart and soul is *unrighteous*.

Unrighteousness is the "norm" east of Eden. To say that we are "unrighteous" is to affirm that we are stuck in the middle of the cycle of sin, shame, and addiction and that we are helplessly spiraling away from God's original design for our lives. Our problem is not that God is running away from us, but that we are running away from God. Our great need is not to try harder than we currently are or for some new bit of spiritual teaching. What we need is God's forgiveness and for an invitation to come back home.

People will sometimes ask me, "If God is love, can't God just forgive?" The problem in this question is the word *just*. People tend to assume that God's pardon is a "small matter" and that it is an easy thing for God to "just" gloss over our sins. And I suppose that if God were *just* "energy" or a good vibe that it *would be easy* for Him to forgive us. But the God of the Bible is personal. God is more like a Father than He is a senile, benevolent grandfather. God is more like a Mother concerned with how her children grow up than like a grandmother who gives us ice cream cones when we visit. God is more like a Spouse who wants to get naked with us than a friend who wants to "talk sports." God is a person, and when *real persons* are betrayed they do not "just forgive." When people hurt us, it is impossible to simply pretend that the betrayal never happened. "Just forgiving" someone that hurts us isn't how reality works in the realm of intimate, personal relationships.

Consider the example of a wife that betrays her husband in some way. The husband has two options. One option would be to retaliate. He can rub her nose in the dirt, tell her she is awful, tell their kids she is awful, and tell all their mutual friends what a horrible wife she has been and what a mistake he made in marrying her. He can drag her through a messy divorce, get a shark for an attorney, and not "fight fair." Option one is to *make her pay*. This we commonly call revenge.

The second option would be to forgive the wife who hurt him. But consider what this will cost the husband. The betrayed husband will have to absorb the pain. It is unrealistic to think that the husband can pretend that his wife did not betray him or pray away the pain. If the husband chooses to forgive his wife, he is at the same time making a choice to absorb the pain and to take the agony of his wife's betrayal into the center of his heart. Practically speaking, those are his only two options. He can return the pain, which we call revenge. Or he can absorb the pain, which we call forgiveness. But forgiveness never "just" happens. It happens when someone chooses to absorb all the pain that comes with being betrayed by someone they love instead of choosing to hurt them back. Forgiveness is not shooting back when others shoot us.

The reason God cannot *just* forgive us has more to do with how real relationships work than with anything else. True forgiveness always costs the forgiver something. That's why forgiveness is a virtue. Forgiveness is hard and it hurts. And the greater the offense, the harder it is to forgive. That is why we cannot "just forgive." Why should God, whose image we reflect, be any different?

The point of all this is to say that I do not believe that our deep feelings of unworthiness are a mere fiction of our mind that we can just "get over." The post-Genesis 3 gap between God and us is real. We *are* unrighteous. The tragedy of Genesis 3 is that the man and woman are *really* barred from God's paradise. It's not just in our heads. Somehow, in some way, at some time, in some form, *it happened*. As the author of Genesis recounts, God "drove out the man; and at the east of the garden of Eden he placed the cherubim, and a sword flaming and turning to guard the way to the tree of life" (Gen 3:24).

Genesis' portrayal of humanity barred from Eden doesn't represent a wrecked mental state but a wrecked cosmic one. All mental confusion, self-esteem issues, shame, violence, addiction, gossip, disappointment, depression, and every fight or heartbreak we've ever experienced are mere symptoms of the real problem: a *real, wrecked relationship between God and us exists* that, until repaired, will reap havoc in our world and in our lives as our shame intensifies, solidifies, and increasingly comes to define our thinking, feeling, and acting.

The Justice of the World

The traditional word for God's response to human sin is "wrath," which is an Old English word for anger. For the longest time whenever I heard God had "wrath," it conjured up images of some ill-tempered madman flying off the handle and "going postal." But the Greek word translated wrath, which is *paradidomi*, merely means to "permit or allow."

Sin is a destructive and addictive out-of-control spiral away from our original design, and "wrath" is what happens when God refuses to step in and stop the process. Wrath is God permitting the destructive spiral to do what it does best—*destroy*. As Paul Achtemeier explains, "The wrath which God visits on sinful humanity consists in simply letting humanity have its own way. The punishment of sin is therefore simply—sin!"[4]

Wrath isn't what happens when God gets his hand on a bottle of Beam and has a particularly pissy day. Let's avoid the traditional caricatures please. Rather, wrath is God leaving us to stew in our own juices and to reap what we've sown. So you might say a "paradidomi shift" is needed when it comes to how

---

4 Paul Achtemeier, *Romans* (Louisville, KY: John Knox Press, 1985), 40.

we understand God's anger. The *worst* thing God could ever do to us is to leave us to our own devices.

Yet it's quite humbling to consider that God is well within God's rights to do just that—a lesson I learned not in seminary but in business school. The rule that governs life in our world's economy is simple. *We pay our own debt.* "Paying our own debt" is the principle our entire justice system is based on as well. When the court sentenced John for committing murder, we called that "paying his debt to society" and no one batted an eye.

Christianity does not make sense apart from an honest acknowledgment that we have all accrued a massive moral debt against God. We were created to love God and to love people, but we have denied that noble calling to serve the addictions of our ego. Our lives are spinning out of control. Each and every day, as we live for ourselves, our debt grows a little bit more. Day after day our addictions harden and God seems a bit more distant. We are like a man with eighty-three credit cards, no limit, no income, a 26 percent interest rate, and an endless appetite for "stuff." Our debt is mounting. John is not the only one on trial. We all are, and deep down we all know the verdict.

Grace

C. S. Lewis was once asked by a group of his colleagues at Oxford about the uniqueness of Christianity. "All religions present ethical challenges. Other religions have stories of virgin births and miracles of gods walking the earth. So *what*," they sneered, "makes Christianity any different?" "What makes Christianity different?" Lewis asked rhetorically before giving his one-word response: GRACE.

Christianity is about grace. Whereas wrath is what happens when God refuses to "step in," grace is what happens when God *does* step in. Grace is a one-way street. It is God's one-way love breathed into a spiritual corpse. Grace is what resurrects us. It is not God meeting us halfway, or picking up the part of the tab we can't afford to pay. Grace is God paying *all of it*. We can no more pay off the moral debt we owe God by "being a good person" than we could pay off our mortgage by throwing a few pennies at a bank teller. But the good news of Christianity is that Jesus Christ has stepped in and done something on our behalf.

We do well to remember that the word *gospel* does not mean "good advice" or "good teaching" or "good life strategy." The word gospel means "good news." Christianity is news about something that has changed the entire course of the cosmos. This is why Christianity is different from every other religious system that has ever or will ever be known to man. Christianity is about grace. Grace is about God climbing down into the darkness and rescuing us from the avalanche. It's about God "stepping in" to rescue our wrecked world. Literally. The logos became flesh, stepped in, and dwelt among us.

The consistent witness of the New Testament links the grace God bestows on us to Jesus' death on the cross. St. Paul speaks of Jesus' death as "a sacrifice of atonement" (Rom 3:25). The author of Hebrews calls Jesus' death "a sacrifice of atonement for the sins of the people" (Heb 2:17). John speaks of Jesus as "the atoning sacrifice for our sins" (1 Jn 2:2). The Greek work translated "atone" means "to pacify God's wrath." The point being made is that Jesus has done something to absolve us from the withdrawing anger of God. That's why the cross is a divine intervention. Jesus stepped in to feel the full brunt of God's anger so that you and I do not have to. Christianity is about grace.

Is God *Really* Angry?

I find that people struggle with the idea that a God of love could be angry with us in the first place. And I fully understand why. Our experience of anger is so broken and shot through with self-centeredness and pride that it's doubtful we *can* grasp what righteous anger looks like. As Eugene Peterson explains, "Anger as an honest manifestation of revealed love, or offended righteousness, is rare among us. We encounter it mostly as a kind of petty irritation, a tantrum, a mean streak coming out when we don't get our own way."[5] We are right to be cautious in speaking of God's anger. We must not take our broken experience of anger and project that onto God. God's anger is much purer than ours.

But the concept of God's anger is important. If God *is* love, then something else must also be true at the same time. Namely, God can feel hurt, betrayed, and wounded. In other words, because God loves, *God* must *also* experience anger when that love is betrayed and rejected. And God's anger is *"always* evidence of his concern."[6] As Abraham Heschel put it, "God's concern is the prerequisite and source of His anger. It is because He cares for man that His anger may be kindled against man."[7]

And so when it comes to God's "anger," let us not glibly remark, "God's above all that." Real relationships follow certain principles. God is not "above all that" because God is not above investing deeply in an intimate relationship with us. God is not angry with us because He doesn't care. God is angry with us precisely because God *does* care. It is the people we love the most that have the greatest capacity to break our hearts. Adam and Eve broke God's heart. Their story is our story. Our addictions break God's heart, too. It happens.

From Curse to Blessing

God not only feels deep anger at the addictive and destructive spiral we are all caught up in. God is also angry at the ways we perpetuate that cycle. And the worst thing God could ever do

---

5 Eugene Peterson, *Five Smooth Stones for Pastoral Work* (Grand Rapids, MI: Eerdmans Publishing Company, 1992), 130.
6 Ibid., 130.
7 Abraham Heschel, *The Prophets* (New York: Harper & Row, 1962), 283.

to express his "wrath" (paradidomi) would be to write us off and leave us to our devices to reap what we've sown.

And so here's the mind shift that I believe needs to be made. The word *paradidomi* is actually the *most* hope-filled word in the New Testament. After all, the Christian Gospel, or good news, is not that we are "handed over" to pay our *own* debt. That would not be good news at all. The Christian Gospel is that Jesus Christ was "handed over" to experience the full weight of our sins on our behalf. "He himself bore our sins in his body on the cross," writes the author of 1 Peter (2:24). We need not pay our own debt. Jesus Christ stepped in and has paid our debt for us.

From whence is our worthiness to come? It is *this belief* that has the power to change our lives. It is this belief that is the basis of our worthiness before God and each other. Once we see something, we cannot un-see it. Jesus being "handed over" for us is all over the Bible. Judas, we are told, sought "an opportunity to betray (paradidomi) [Jesus] . . . when no crowd was present" (Lk 22:6). The Jewish leadership "handed him over (paradidomi) to be condemned to death" (Lk 24:20). In a similar manner, Pilate, after having Jesus flogged, "handed him over (paradidomi) to be crucified" (Mk 15:15). Since Jesus' crucifixion is providential, God also "gave him up (paradidomi) for all of us" (Rom 8:32). Of course, God did not drag Jesus to the cross against his will. On the contrary, the "Son of God . . . loved me and gave himself (paradidomi) for me" (Gal 2:20).

Jesus' crucifixion was not an accident or an "oops." The cross is the means by which God has reconciled us to Himself. This is the good news of the Christian Gospel. Jesus Christ was "handed over" for us. This was God's sentence on human sin. The Judge was judged for us. The anger of God fell upon Jesus. You and I are free.

The Cup of God's Anger

Jesus often spoke of his death symbolically in terms of his "cup." For instance, two of Jesus' disciples once asked Him for a place of prominence in His Kingdom. Jesus responded with a question of his own: "Are you able to drink the cup that I am about to drink?" (Mt 20:22). In the same way, the night before Jesus dies he is terrified of "the cup" that awaits him and asks His Father to "remove" it (Mk 14:36).

The "cup" was an Old Testament symbol for the anger of God. According to Isaiah, "at the hand of the Lord" is "the cup of his wrath" (Isa 51:17). In a similar manner, Jeremiah symbolically takes from God's "hand [the] cup . . . of wrath" (Jer 25:15), which Ezekiel names "a cup of horror and desolation" (Ezek 23:33). According to Habakkuk, when one drinks "the cup in the Lord's right hand . . . shame [overtakes] glory" (Hab 2:16). As John Stott explains:

> The cup from which [Jesus] shrank . . . symbolized . . . the spiritual agony of bearing the sins of the world—in other words, of enduring the divine judgment that those sins deserved. Old Testament imagery will have been well known to Jesus. He must have recognized the cup he was being offered as containing the wine of God's wrath.[8]

Here we see clearly the "grace" that makes Christianity unique. Rather than allowing us to experience the full weight of our addictive and destructive behavior, God, in Christ, steps in and experiences the full weight of our sins *for* us and *with* us. Put differently, living east of Eden places us under a curse. "Christ redeemed us . . . by becoming a curse for us" (Gal 3:13). By nature, we know nothing but sin. "For our

---

8 John Stott, *The Cross of Christ* (Downers Grove, IL: Intervarsity Press, 2006), 78–79.

sake" God made Jesus "to *be sin* who knew no sin" (2 Cor 5:21, italics mine). In God's wrath, we are "handed over" to death. Jesus, however, "was handed over to death for our trespasses" (Rom 4:25).

It is helpful to think of both sin and salvation as a "substitution" of sorts. Sin is the addictive process of using loincloths of our own making as substitutes for God. The beauty of salvation is that God, in Christ, substitutes himself for us by dying on a cross. We are addicted to clothing ourselves. Jesus intervened and was stripped. Christianity is about grace. The word Gospel means good news.

Avoiding Caricatures: What the Cross Is Not

It saddens me to consider how much Jesus' sacrificial death has been distorted and caricatured. The typical conservative error is to couch the crucifixion in terms of Divine Child Abuse, which might go something like this: "God is fed up with our behavior and needs someone to torture—because somehow torture is what God's holiness demands. Jesus steps in for us. We can avoid God's torture by accepting Jesus, which will enable us to sneak into heaven's back door when we die." This just isn't the Christian Gospel. Jesus doesn't want to be accepted. He wants to be embraced.

Of course, the liberal error is equally as silly, whereby the cross is seen as nothing more than the full expression of God's love. If I wanted to express to my beloved wife Emily how deeply I love her, I think the last thing I would do is throw myself in front of a train to prove a point. That is not love. It is suicide. The cross wasn't God's last effort to "get through" to our world. The cross was the culmination of God's plan to abolish sin, shame, and death. The cross is the deepest truth we are invited to "see" about God. It is also the deepest truth we are invited to "see" about ourselves.

I say all this because Jesus' sacrifice on the cross is far too beautiful to get wrong, misunderstand, or ignore. It is true that Jesus' act of "taking our place" is *mysterious*. I know the idea *sounds* simple. But the cross is anything but simple. Forgiveness is a complex, cosmic problem; salvation entails a complex, cosmic solution.

Such is why I am convinced that what we say about Jesus' sacrificial death *for us* will always be inadequate. Jesus was fully God and fully human. The logos was God *and* the logos was with God before entering our world. This means that the cross was not *merely* the plan of the human Jesus—as if Jesus had to wrestle our salvation from an unwilling, capricious Father who would probably prefer to leave us alone if Jesus wasn't so bent on saving us. Nor was the cross *solely* the Father's idea—as if the Father had to beat and bruise His unwilling Son for the mistakes of the world. As John Stott explains:

> We must never make Christ the object of God's punishment or God the object of Christ's persuasion, for both God and Christ were subjects not objects, taking the initiative together to save sinners. The Father did not lay on the Son an ordeal he was reluctant to bear, nor did the Son extract from the Father a salvation he was reluctant to bestow.[9]

Stott's point is that the work of God and Christ cannot be separated, for "*in Christ* God was reconciling the world to himself" (2 Cor 5:19, italics mine). Reconciliation is the work of the Divine Society we call the Trinity.

A Final Meal

We see Jesus' work in obedience to His Father most clearly the night before his death. Jesus eats the Passover meal with His

---

9 Stott, *The Cross of Christ*, 151.

disciples. Commonly called the Last Supper, this is where "the Lord's Supper," "Communion," "Eucharist," and "the Mass" come from in Christian worship. So central was this meal to Jesus' first followers that even today most Christians commemorate Jesus by some form of liturgical or ritual reenactment of this meal. But it is important to recall that the first Eucharist was a Passover meal,[10] which was already a longstanding Jewish tradition.

The Passover was the Jewish celebration that recalled God's mighty act of rescuing Israel from Egyptian slavery. But the Passover functioned less as a memorial of the past than as a hopeful expectation that God's new world would finally dawn in the future. Devout Jews in Jesus' day were waiting for a day when God's Kingdom would arrive on earth once and for all. In God's new world, people will beat their "swords into plowshares" and their "spears into pruning hooks" (Isa 2:4). God will return to walk with humanity in the cool of the day, and the world will be put right once and for all.

In God's new world, life on earth will be like a wonderful party. Justice and peace will be the norm. The curse of Eden will be reversed. "Then the Lord God will wipe away the tears from all faces" (Isa 25:8). This hope *is* what the Passover was really about—that one day, pain and tears would be abolished for good, and that God and humanity would stand reconciled and naked in Eden. The Passover was about a future, cosmic freedom that only God Himself could bring about. It was about the birth of God's new world.

And so with that in mind it's interesting to ponder what Jesus was up to in this final meal with His disciples the night before He died. Jesus wanted his disciples to understand that Israel's history was about to reach its climax in and through something that He alone will do. Jesus' mission is to completely

---

10 In Mark, Luke, and Matthew, it is a Passover meal. In John, it happens one night earlier while the lambs are being slaughtered (assuming they ate the night of the foot washing).

remove the slavery of humanity's shame and to restore them to a place of worthiness before God. It will culminate in Jesus' atoning death on the cross. A *second exodus,* a much bigger jail-break than ever before, will take place. But this time it won't be from Egypt, but from the pharaoh of sin, shame, and death that has kept humanity shackled for far too long.

> While they were eating, Jesus took a loaf of bread, and after blessing it he broke it, gave it to his disciples, and said, "Take, eat; this is my body." Then he took a cup, and after giving thanks he gave it to them, saying, "Drink from it, all of you; for this is my blood of the covenant, which is poured out for many for the for-giveness of sins" (Mt 26:26–28).[11]

It is significant that Jesus identifies the loaf of bread with his own body. As bread nourishes one's physical life, Jesus' death is meant to sustain the Christian's spiritual life. Forgiveness of sins is now accessible through Jesus' death. He paid the debt necessary to free us from our exile.

Our shame has been removed and our worthiness before God has been restored. The party of God has arrived. We are no longer in need of loincloths. There is no more need to cover up. Through the merits of Jesus' cross, new clothes are given to us so that we can come before our King once again and celebrate.

Invited to the Party

Jesus often compared the coming of God's Kingdom to a mas-sive, joy-filled party. He told one parable in particular about a King that throws a wedding banquet for his son and about how all the guests, who have already mailed in their RSVP "yes," changed their mind and "made light of it" (Mt 22:5). The king's

---

11 See also Mk 14:22–24 and Lk 22:17–19, as well as 1 Cor 11:23–25.

heart is grieved. "The wedding is ready," the king says, "but those invited were *not* worthy" (Mt 22:8, italics mine). So the king issues a decree.

> "Go therefore into the main streets, and invite everyone you find to the wedding banquet." Those slaves went out into the streets and gathered all whom they found, both good and bad; so the wedding hall was filled with guests. But when the king came in to see the guests, he noticed a man there who was not wearing a wedding robe, and he said to him, "Friend, how did you get in here without a wedding robe?" And he was speechless. Then the king said to the attendants, "Bind him hand and foot, and throw him into the outer darkness, where there will be weeping and gnashing of teeth." For many are called, but few are chosen. (Mt 22:9–14)

It is significant that everyone is invited to the party. Not one person is excluded.

The guests are gathered in from the "main streets," a clear indication that this group is diverse. The guests are diverse economically (rich and poor), racially (Jew and Gentile), and morally (good and bad). No one is excluded from the banquet, save that one man not wearing his robe.

That all the other guests were wearing wedding robes also tells us something significant. The King decided to provide new clothes to all of his guests at the door. After all, the guests are coming right off the streets. There was no time to run over to David's Bridal and buy one. The poor guests would not have been able to afford a wedding robe anyway. And so the King in Jesus' parable provides wedding robes to each of his guests at his *own* expense. One man, however, refused the king's gift. He was under the impression that he could approach the king just as he was.

New Clothes

From whence is our worth to come? The wedding robe represents a life of utter dependence on Jesus Christ, which implies a commitment to find our worth, salvation, and peace not in our story but in His story. We cannot rely on anything we do but must rest on what God in Christ has done for us. Hearing the verdict, we joyfully throw ourselves at the mercy of God's Court where *He pays what we owe.* Unless we come to the banquet on the king's terms, we remain "not worthy" and our life is spent dressing ourselves in loincloths of our own making, which is so terribly exhausting. Only when we ask the King of Creation to dress us in the new clothes that Jesus provides will anything in our life begin to change.

It is actually quite remarkable how frequently the Bible uses the image of "new clothes" to speak of the salvation and restoration that are offered us through Jesus Christ. As Isaiah prophesied long ago, "I will greatly rejoice in the Lord, my whole being shall exult in my God; for *he has clothed me* with the garments of salvation, he has covered me with the *robe of righteousness,* as a bridegroom decks himself with a garland, and as a bride adorns herself with her jewels" (Isa 61:10, italics mine). Picking up on this theme, St. Paul urges the Ephesians "to clothe yourselves with the new self" (Eph 4:24), which happens when we "put on the Lord Jesus Christ" (Rom 13:14). Revelation puts it, find "white robes to clothe you and to keep the shame of your nakedness from being seen" (Rev 3:18). We later read that one can only put on God's robe when they "have washed their robes and made them white in the blood of the Lamb" (Rev 7:14). New clothes await us all at the foot of Jesus' cross.

The Invitation

The good news of the Christian Gospel is that God offers us a completely new wardrobe, a metaphor for a new sense of *worthiness, righteousness, and restored intimacy with God.* But far too often we settle for less. The wedding robe is intimidating. It represents a life of utter dependence on Jesus Christ—a return to Eden where we stand naked before God and each other and where we trust that God's commands are meant to increase our joy and not diminish it.

Learning to put on God's new clothes, or being formed as a Christian, is about moving from a self-centered focus to a God-centered focus; from autonomy to obedience; from independence to discipleship. It is not about taking off secular loincloths and putting on religious loincloths. It is not about getting serious about "the Law." It's about getting serious about Love. It's about learning from Jesus how to come more fully alive because, well, we already have been raised to new life.

Yet we are so suspicious of this invitation! After all, we westerners define freedom *as* autonomy and independence. We are threatened by the news that God defines freedom much differently than we do. And so in our suspicion we settle for less. At worst we unapologetically decide to live for ourselves. "Let us eat and drink," we say, "for tomorrow we die" (1 Cor 15:32). And at best we roll up our sleeves and resolve to do our Christian "duty." We come to church. We say our prayers. We give some money. But then we go back to looking out for number one.

In *Mere Christianity,* C. S. Lewis claims that what keeps us from a much deeper life of faith is our tendency to talk about our *self* as the starting point, with its desires and interests, and then to talk about this completely different thing called *morality,* which usually conflicts with what "I" want. "I want to eat the forbidden fruit. Morality says the fruit is off limits. Looks like I've got to choose between being good and being happy!" This seems to be how most of us understand our dilemma. The impact of this is that in an effort to be "good" (however we define goodness, because when independence is our primary value we always get to define "what's good" for ourselves), we will sometimes sacrifice what *we want* to do the "right" thing. We wake up early to go to church as opposed to sleeping in, or we give some money to charity instead of buying a nicer car. And then we hope that "being good" doesn't cost us too much money or energy or pride to get on with the real work of living our *life*. But this is not the Christian way at all. As Lewis puts it:

> The Christian way is different; harder, and easier. Christ says, "Give me all. I don't want so much of your time and so much of your money and so much of your work: I want you. I have not come to torment your natural self, but to kill it. I don't want to cut off a branch here and there, I want the whole tree down. Hand over the whole natural self. I will give you a new self instead. In fact, I will give you Myself: my own will shall become yours.[12]

Here we have the essence of the divine invitation to clothe ourselves with Jesus Christ. A "new self" and Jesus' "own will" are offered. That's the invitation. The old you drowned in the waters of baptism. A new self is hidden with Christ in God. The invitation is to get to know the self that God knows.

God does not offer us tips for a better life, nor is Jesus like a really good vitamin we take for a "daily boost." But God does offer us His *own* life, which is always experienced as abundant life. If Jesus truly is the "King's son," it is a silly thing to invite Him into our life as a self-help coach, an encourager, or as anything other than a liberating King worthy of our complete devotion in every aspect of our life. "The Christian way is different," Lewis says. It isn't about becoming a nice self. It's about becoming a completely new self.

---

12 Lewis, *Mere Christianity*, 197.

Where Change Begins

We do not become a new self by exerting our will power or by trying really, really hard to change. Christianity is about grace. God invites us to cultivate a new willingness to follow the Spirit's call, not to try harder to be a better person. The new clothes God offers us are not something we merit or purchase. The wedding robe is a gift that Jesus purchases for us.

We need look no further than the cross to know just how much that gift cost. On the cross, God, in the person of Jesus Christ, absorbed all the sin, anxiety, guilt, shame, tragedy, and heartbreak of the human race: past, present, and future. There is no pain, fear, grief, or experience of shame that God is not acquainted with. Jesus has experienced all of it.

We recall that it is impossible to "just forgive." When one is wounded he can either absorb the pain or return the pain. The miracle of Christianity is that on the cross, God, in Christ, chose to absorb the cosmic pain of the entire exiled creation. "It" has already been dealt with fully—the pain you've caused others, the pain others have caused you, and the seemingly meaningless tragedies that perpetually plague our world. Jesus absorbed all of it. God is no longer angry.

The Justice of God

We began this chapter by looking at the justice that governs life in our world—the principle that says "we pay our own debt." I pray that we see and never un-see again how different and magnificent the justice is that governs life in God's world, which is seen most clearly in Jesus Christ, fully God and fully human, paying our debt for us on the cross. Our debt has been paid in full. New clothes have been purchased. The party has begun. This is the wonderful justice of God.

We don't need to spend our lives spiraling away from God out of a deep sense of unworthiness and shame. Our worthiness—that critically important piece that gives us access to love and belonging—lives inside of *Jesus'* story. Our true life and new self are hidden in Him. He was stripped naked so that we might be clothed.

Our Day in Court

St. Paul writes, "All of us must appear before the judgment seat of Christ" (2 Cor 5:10). Like John in the courtroom, we will all find ourselves before the divine bench. From whence is our worthiness to come? Do we dare go before the King in an orange jumpsuit, or will we don the wedding robe that Christ has provided at His own great expense?

Christianity is about the grace of Jesus *stepping in*. There is something powerful inside of Jesus' story that can erase our every mistake, scrub away our shame, give us the resources to change, and help us know for the first time that we are completely worthy of love and belonging. And that something is the *cross*. On the cross, God, in Christ, chose to absorb the pain, feel the pain, and to take the pain of his image-bearer's betrayal into the center of His heart. In and through Jesus' cross, we are invited to approach "the throne of grace with boldness, so that we may receive mercy and find grace" in our time of need (Heb 4:16). In Jesus' cross we have forgiveness and an invitation to come back home. Let us not make light of God's invitation. Our worthiness comes only through the cross of Jesus Christ.

A day will most certainly come when I, John, will stand before the Judge. On that day there will be no shackled, lifeless, and guilty John, for the only "sentence" that matters was issued two thousand years ago. That is what I believe. My verdict has been reached and this verdict will not be overturned. The verdict is not guilty. I am free.

Discussion Questions

1. Do you believe that some people, in God's eyes, are "better" than others with respect to their moral behavior? Why or why not?

2. What does the word "unrighteous" mean to you? What does it mean to say that God gives us His righteousness as a gift?

3. If someone hurts us, are forgiveness and revenge our only options? Is forgiveness always a painful experience for the forgiver?

4. What does the word "grace" mean? Is the concept of grace unique to Christianity?

5. Do you think God's love and God's anger are irreconcilable concepts? Why or why not?

6. Is the "Eucharist" or "Lord's Supper" a significant part of your life? What does it mean to you?

7. How do you understand God's "gracious invitation" to us and to the world? What are we invited to?

CHAPTER 4

A Better Country

A few years ago I traveled to Burma for a month of mission work with a group of seminarians. One of our tasks was to lead a retreat for teenagers from all over the country. These teens were bold and curious. They asked all kinds of questions about us and about the United States. "Are you married or dating someone, and if not, what's your problem?" "What do Americans do for fun?" And since they were about fifteen years behind the latest Hollywood trends, every Burmese teen just had to know the latest scoop on America's most celebrated and talented actor— Arnold Schwarzenegger.

The mood of the retreat was light until one young man raised his hand. He spoke passionately for a few minutes in a language I did not understand. Upon finishing, the translator looked at me somewhat saddened and slightly embarrassed, and told me his question. "Why is it that some people have a soft heart, and other people have a stony heart?"

His name was Pwe Thein, and he had traveled for eighteen hours to be with us from a remote village in Burma full of ethnic tension and political persecution. Pwe Thein had experienced the full weight of what stony hearts could do to his family and to his country. Pwe Thein longed for a better country.

I think we understand his question. After a century shattered by two world wars, the Holocaust, the Atomic bomb, and terrorism, we've come to accept that stony hearts are a reality in our world. We see stony hearts in our co-workers, family, and friends. We encounter them in the people we interact with on a day-to-day basis. Stony hearts are behind every hurtful word, every rude remark, and every critical comment. And if we have the courage to look inward and tell the truth about our condition, we will see stony hearts in ourselves.

I don't believe any of us rationally and consciously choose our stony heart. No child chooses to grow up to be cold or distant or impatient. No adult rationally chooses to be weighed down by the stones of anger and pride and contempt. Our shame-filled, loincloth-addicted world has taught us these things. As we build a life around "covering up," at the same time we inherit unhealthy behaviors and attitudes that over time make our hearts stony.

I'd even go so far as to say that we're born with "stony" inclinations. Anthropologists speak of an ingrained ethnocentrism. Biologists speak of our preservation instinct. Psychologists speak of our shadow side. Theologians speak of original sin. But it matters little *what* we call this "stony heart phenomenon." What matters is that our stony world has formed us into stony people who need to be rescued. We *get* where Pwe Thein's question is coming from. All is not right with our world. We, too, are desperate for a better country.

Wanting More

We know in our bones that something has gone radically wrong with this world. No matter how hard we try to numb our dissatisfaction with the state of our world, eventually a dark cloud of disappointment finds us. Just about anything, it seems, can awaken this sad feeling. We get in a fight with our wife.

Someone we love dies. We get sick or fall short of other people's expectations or get seized by anxiety. Or we just pick up the paper and *read*. We read of war and famine and hurricanes and disease on one page and about the newest life-changing lipstick on the next. Something, we sense, is out of joint.

Or maybe we just walk past a beggar on our way into the pharmacy. He's the seventh beggar we've walked past that day. We are filled with this weird mixture of shame and relief that we have safely evaded him without being asked for money. And *that* makes us want a better world: for the homeless, for the people we love, for ourselves.

I think this deep longing for "something more" starts early in our development. No one ever sits us down and teaches us about injustice or about our desire for rescue. They don't have to. One of the first lessons we learn is that life isn't fair. When I was five years old, I wanted to join a club that my best friend was starting. But Jeffrey, the group's founder, president, and only member, informed me that you had to be 5½ years old to join. And no one had to tell me or teach me what I ended up saying next as I stormed off in tears, "That's not fair."

We may or may not believe that a just world is a possibility, or that God's nudist colony might ever return to the earth we inhabit. But when we look at our world, and our lives, we feel frustration, anger, and anxiety because we want a better world. And what's so frustrating, and what confuses us so much, is that we've learned how to fix just about everything else in the world. Other things break all the time and we *fix* them. My car broke down the other day. I took it to "my guy" Silvio and he fixed it. The next day I got a headache. I took an aspirin and the aspirin "fixed" it.

We can fix cars. We can fix headaches. So why can't we fix our world, our relationships, and our own inner pain? Why can't we climb out of the avalanche? Why can't we rescue *ourselves?*

Longing for Eden

We all carry deep within us a longing for something "more." We don't feel entirely at home in our world. Our most satisfying moments of beauty, accomplishment, and safety fail to satisfy us entirely. Even our most intimate relationships are still characterized by hiding and pretense. We've been kicked out of God's garden and we yearn desperately to go back.

According to C. S. Lewis, our thirst for a better country tells us something profound about *the big why* behind our existence. This is how he puts it in *Mere Christianity*:

> Creatures are not born with desires unless satisfaction for those desires exists. A baby feels hunger: well, there is such a thing as food. A duckling wants to swim: well, there is such a thing as water. Men feel sexual desire: well, there is such a thing as sex. If I find in myself a desire which no experience in this world can satisfy, the most probable explanation is that I was made for another world.[1]

Lewis claims that the reason we feel estranged in this world is because this world in its present form is not our *true home*. We yearn for something more because we exist for something more, and in fact, at least according to the Book of Genesis, used to possess something more. Adam and Eve were completely at home in God's garden and lost that home because of their disobedience. It happened. Our hearts feel that loss in a way that is too deep to describe. Their loss was our loss, too. We long to be at home, once again, with God. Our souls will be forever restless until they finally rest in Him.

---

1 Lewis, *Mere Christianity*, 136–137.

A Chapter on "The End" Dab Smack in "The Middle"

Most Christian books save this chapter on God's plan to rescue the world until the end. After all, a chapter on "heaven" is a comforting way to conclude a work of prose. It feels good to remember that what Gandalf told Sam in *The Lord of the Rings* is what Jesus first told his disciples. "Everything sad will one day come untrue."

But I am persuaded that a clear and compelling vision of God's glorious end, which is the bedrock of the Christian faith, belongs at the forefront of our minds—*especially* if we desire to grow into the salvation we have already received. We cannot talk about God's glorious future as an afterthought. A vision of God's glorious future should inform how we live our lives *now*. This is how Dallas Willard puts it:

> We are greatly strengthened for life in the kingdom now by an understanding of what our future holds, and especially of how that future relates to our present experience. For only then do we really understand what our current life is and are we able to make choices that agree with that reality.[2]

A clear picture of the future that awaits us is an indispensable component to growing into Christian maturity. After all, whatever we place at the center of our life *will* form us. How we imagine this story we call life ends will impact the part we choose to play. If we think life is a meaningless free-for-all, then it only makes sense to place money, work, pleasure, friends, our enemies, our spouse, or perhaps possessions at the center of our life. *They* will be the compasses that guide our life.

---

2 Dallas Willard, *The Divine Conspiracy: Rediscovering Our Hidden Life in God* (San Francisco: Harper, 1998), 387.

But here's why this matters. Whatever we place at the center of our life will inform our choices, which will in turn form our habits, and our habits become cemented in our character. And our character, rather than being dissolved when we die, will in a mystical way be "carried over"—at least in part.

I'm not saying that the character we die with becomes the character we take to "the other side." Nothing could be less hopeful or orthodox than that. As St. Paul explains, "We will all be changed, in a moment, in the twinkling of an eye, at the last trumpet. For the trumpet will sound, and the dead will be raised imperishable, and we will be changed" (1 Cor 15:51–52). However, the Bible often suggests that who we become on earth will have ramifications that extend past our life on earth. I think this is what Paul was getting at when he exhorted the Corinthians to *live wisely,* saying "the work of each builder will become visible, for the Day will disclose it" (1 Cor 3:13). Again, I am not trying to nullify the importance of grace or slip a little "works righteousness" into the conversation. But I am trying to honor what the Bible teaches about the importance of the sort of person we become while here on earth.

Orthodox Christianity has always taught that a "Day of the Lord" is coming and that to live wisely is to align our life *now* with the reality of what God will bring to earth once and for all *later.* We all long for the home God created us for. Wisdom is about anticipating what God's home will be like and cultivating the willingness that allows God's grace to transform us into the sort of person who will feel at home when God's new world does arrive in its fullness. Christians have traditionally called this "preparation process" our sanctification.

A New Day

Our sanctification has a clear referent. We are being sanctified *for* something. God is preparing a new world for *us* and God is preparing us for a new world. This new home has many names in the Bible—the end of exile, the new Eden, eternal life, the new heavens and new earth, the restoration of all things, and the New Jerusalem are among my favorites. But it matters little what we call it. What matters is that we understand God's new world and "change our mind" about aspects of our present life that are out of step with how things will one day fully and finally be for *good*. But to do so there are a few "essentials" we must understand.

It Will Come to Us

God's home will come to us. We do not come to it. Nor can we bring God's new world about ourselves by striving for justice. God's new world will come definitively in the future to this earth as an act of sheer grace. The hope of Christianity is not that we go to heaven when we die. Our hope is that God will give us a glorious, resurrected body just like Jesus' glorious resurrected body.

All this will happen when the curtain on history closes. There is a grand finale that awaits our world. I imagine most of us will die before this happens. If this should happen, our spirit will depart to be with Christ. Paul even says this state is "far better" than life on earth (Phil 1:23). However, this state between our death and the restoration of all things is *a* better country, but not *the* better country. Whatever we experience immediately after we die, i.e., "heaven," will be like a really good appetizer for what is to come. But let us not confuse "heaven" with the feast. The feast happens when God recreates the earth and dwells amongst *us*. John the Seer records his vision of God's glorious grand finale in the Book of Revelation.

> I saw the holy city, the new Jerusalem, coming down out of heaven from God, prepared as a bride adorned for her husband. And I heard a loud voice from the

throne saying, "See, the home of God is among mortals. He will dwell with them; they will be his peoples, and God himself will be with them; he will wipe away every tear from their eyes. Death will be no more; mourning and crying and pain will be no more, for the first things have passed away." And the one who was seated on the throne said, "See, I am making all things new." (Rev 21:2–5)

This earth is not a petri dish where God is growing true believers he plans to one day zap to some other realm. Nor will the earth be discarded when the trumpet on history sounds. God will recreate it. The knowledge, presence, and beauty of God will fill this earth as the water fills the seas. Think about that next time you're tempted to litter. The cosmos is a massive temple.

Imagining the Unimaginable

I fear this isn't how most of us imagine the world ending. "Well, I guess the sun will burn up the earth, but I'll be long dead by then," people say. Or maybe "the crazies," as one person I know calls fundamentalists, have frightened you with their fiery images of burning lakes and five-headed frog monsters coming to earth to slaughter the unbelievers. I believe that the Bible invites us to imagine and build our lives around a more hopeful sort of ending.

I don't mean to imply that God's justice arriving on earth will be a comforting experience for all people. In fact, the Bible suggests just the opposite. But we who stake our lives on the goodness of God are invited to stretch our minds and imagine the unimaginable. It's a paradox. The Bible says that eye hasn't seen nor ear heard what God has in store for those who love Him (1 Cor 2:9). Peter says that even the angels are desperate to know what God has in store for our world. Not even the angels know for sure what a restored creation might look like. St. Paul says that *at best* we see in a mirror dimly (1 Cor 13:12). Yet the One on the throne still commands us to *see* that He makes all things new on this earth.

Material

Life after death is not about heaven and harps and going to church in the clouds. God's Kingdom will certainly be a *spiritual* realm in the sense that God's Spirit will be the air we breathe. However, we will have glorious new *bodies*. I expect representatives from the animal kingdom to be present as well. They were, after all, "saved" when God told Noah to make an ark.[3] That "small salvation" points to a grander feast God will bring about at the end of history. There will be food, wine, laughter, and dancing (except for *line dancing*, for "nothing accursed will be found there any more"). We will experience something more real than anything we've ever experienced before. *We* will be more real than ever before.

Matter is good. God created it. God saw fit to enter a human body. Matter is not unspiritual or dirty. I don't know if there will be toilets, airplanes, or different seasons in God's Kingdom. Like Paul, I see dimly in a mirror. But the home Jesus is at work recreating even now will be material, real, solid, spiritual, and glorious. This is how Timothy Keller describes it:

> This world is not simply a theatre for individual conversion narratives, to be discarded at the end when we all go to heaven. No, the ultimate purpose of Jesus is not only individual salvation and pardon for sins but also the renewal of this world, the end of disease, poverty, injustice, violence, suffering and death. The climax of history is not a higher form of disembodied

---

3 If you are unfamiliar with this story, read Genesis, chapters 6–8.

consciousness but a feast. God made the world with all its colors, tastes, lights, sounds, with all its life-forms living in interdependent systems. It is now marred, stained, and broken, and he will not rest until he has put it right.[4]

No religion is more concerned with the state of our material world than Christianity. It baffles me when people skeptically object that Jesus never could have violated the natural order by curing the sick and healing the blind. They're missing the point. Christians don't believe Jesus ever did anything *against* nature. His "miracles" weren't a violation of the natural order. They were a restoration of the natural order.

I submit that it is *we* that are not normal. We are not fully human like Jesus was. To long for a better country is to long for *normalcy*. We long for our life and our world to conform to "God's norm." Truly, God's ways are not ours. We long for our stony ways to change.

Intimacy Restored

We also will come alive for the very first time when God re-creates our world and us. Humans are, after all, the pinnacles of creation. God's new day will be a personal and intimate experience for each person involved. We will know ourselves for the very first time. In fact, we will know ourselves as God has known us all along. We will finally love ourselves as God has loved us.

The Book of Revelation gives us a wonderful image of what the "new normal" will be. "Nothing accursed will be found there any more. But the throne of God and of the Lamb will be in it, and his servants will worship him; they will see his face, and his name will be on their foreheads" (Rev 22:3–4).

---

4 Keller, *The Prodigal God*, 124.

I believe this is the most intimate, vulnerable, and loving image in the Bible. We will return to the nudist colony. We will stand cleansed before the God that cleanses us. We will know God, each other, and ourselves fully, and we will not experience shame. Only intimacy and joy will remain.

Community Restored

This doesn't mean that God's salvation will be a private experience. Everything worthwhile in life is to be shared. God's new world will work the same way. Salvation is certainly personal but by no means is it private. Jesus doesn't save individual persons. Jesus saves the Church, of which you and I are a part. Jesus also saves the entire creation.

We will "all get along" in God's new creation. Each one of us will play an indispensable part in each other's lives as God intended us to do from the beginning. We will be truly interdependent.

We've all had glimpses of how wonderful this can be. Certain people have the gift of bringing out hidden aspects of our personality. I think that's why "empty nests" can be so startling at first. Rather than having "more" of each other, a husband and wife have less of each other when their youngest leaves. Their youngest put them both in touch with a playful part of themselves that they have forgotten how to bring out in each other. "The more the merrier" is a guiding principle in the Kingdom of God.

Creative, Meaningful Work Restored

Such is why we will all engage, once again, in meaningful and creative work. We will all joyfully play the part God designed us to play. God's new world will not be boring. There will be plenty to do. No two people will have the same skill set. As

I write this book, I am mildly freaking out because *I will be out of a job*. I am a minister. My job is to help people know God. But in God's new world we will all know God, from the least of us to the greatest.

Jesus told a parable about how his servants that prove faithful in this life will be given more responsibility in the next. "Well done, good and trustworthy slave," the Master says, "you have been trustworthy in a few things, I will put you in charge of *many things*; enter into the joy of your master" (Mt 25:21).

The joy of God's new world will involve a vocation, or calling, for each of us. The Bible hints of our newfound responsibility in a million different ways. St. Paul says we will be judging angels (1 Cor 6:3). Jesus says we'll be on thrones judging the twelve tribes of Israel (Mt 19:28). The point being made is that we will have responsibility. There will be creative and meaningful work to do under the Sovereign Lordship of God. The glory of God's new world will be that it is never fully completed. That is why St. Paul says that in God's new world only three things will be left: faith, hope, and love (1 Cor 13:13). Paul says that even in a perfect world where our soul is at rest, we will still live by faith and hope—not faith and hope that God will "fix" anything, but that God's glory and peace and wisdom will expand more and more and more in us and through us for eternity. Each day in God's new world will be a new chapter, each one better than before. The book will never end. The Author of Life will never stop writing.

The Hinge

There is, of course, a belief Christians hold, without which none of this makes sense. We believe in the bodily resurrection of Jesus Christ from the dead. As St. Paul once put it, "If Christ has not been raised, your faith is futile," and, "If for this life only we have hoped in Christ, we are of all people most to be pitied" (see 1 Cor 15:17–19).

Paul insists that Jesus' resurrection from the dead is everything. If Jesus is still dead, so are we. Our hope for a renewed world where we're back in the garden hinges on the truth of Jesus' resurrection. The reason the first Christians were so confident in God's renewed creation was because they saw a prototype of that world in Jesus' resurrected body.

Easter is a window into the better country we so deeply long for. The Bible says that when Jesus is revealed, which is a reference to His Second Coming, "we will be like him, for we will see him as he is" (1 Jn 3:2). And what we see in Jesus' resurrection is a different sort of body. He had a body that wasn't restrained by time or space. And yet it was very much a *real* body. In fact, it was more real than his earthly body. At the heart of our hope is that Jesus "will transform the body of our humiliation that it may be conformed to the body of his glory" (Phil 3:21). There will be so much to do in God's new world and so much to experience. We're all going to be in need of a new and better body. We'll need an upgrade. That's what our hope in the resurrection is all about.

The Big Why Revisited

We began by looking at a question we cannot escape. To be human is to ask *why*. Why are we here? Why did God create us? A recent *Newsweek* article describes the centrality of this question.

The thirst for God is still there. How could it not be, when the profoundest human questions—*Why does the universe exist rather than nothing? How did humanity come to be on this remote blue speck of a planet? What happens to us after death?*—remain as pressing and mysterious as they've always been?[5]

It is important to be as clear as possible. God's new world *is* itself the answer to *the big why*. We were created to play an indispensable role in God's new heavens and new earth under the Lordship of Jesus Christ.

Longing for a Better Country

I believe that our longings for a better country are the key to our personal transformation. The Bible begins with the human race forfeiting their home in God's garden. It then climaxes with Jesus leaving His *home* at the Father's side to live and die as a human. The Bible culminates with God restoring humanity's home through the merits and grace of Jesus Christ. That is why faith *in* Jesus is at the heart of Christian discipleship. He alone is "the gate" to the mansion being prepared for us (see Jn 10:9, 14:3).

But the longings themselves are the keys to our transformation. Our longing for more is what drives us, for good or for ill. What we do with the deep longings of our soul will either ruin us or prepare us for eternal glory. The question is not whether or not we long for a better country. The question is always *where are we looking?*

Perhaps no author of the Bible lays out the path to faithfulness more clearly than the author of Hebrews. Here we are given a clear picture of what it means to live by faith. Speaking of "the faithful" he writes:

> They confessed that they were strangers and foreigners
> on the earth, for people who speak in this way make
> it clear that they are seeking a homeland. If they

---

5 Andrew Sullivan, "The Forgotten Jesus." *Newsweek* (April 9, 2012). I do not commend the primary message of this article, but quote Sullivan here to emphasize just how much the *big why* presses upon secularist and religious alike.

had been thinking of the land that they left behind, they would have had opportunity to return. But as it is, they desire a better country, that is, a heavenly one. Therefore God is not ashamed to be called their God; indeed, he has prepared a city for them. (Heb 11:13–16)

Faithfulness is about living in this world with both eyes fixed on God's Kingdom. The Biblical invitation to find our deepest identity in the Kingdom of God, and not the Kingdom of the World, is on every page of the Bible. We can build a life around anything. Honestly, we can. The great invitation, the essence of God's Party, is to build a life around the God and Father of our Lord Jesus Christ, for He has built His life *around us.*

Anticipating our Hope in God's New World

But to build our life around God we must anticipate our hope in God's new world. To anticipate something means to realize something ahead of time. To anticipate God's new world is to speak, think, and act now in a way that is consistent with our belief that a new world is coming.

Consider the man who puts on a raincoat while the sun is still shining because he anticipates that it is going to rain later. He dresses now in a way that is appropriate for the future reality that he expects. When the rain arrives he wants to be ready for it.

A transformed heart is like that raincoat. A person committed to having their stony heart transformed into a soft heart is like that man anticipating the rain. I believe that a day is coming when God's truth, mercy, grace, and justice will pour down like rain and flood our earth. On that day "the earth will be filled with the knowledge of the glory of the Lord, as the waters cover the sea" (Hab 2:14).

"Why is it," Pwe Thein wanted to know, "that some people have a soft heart, and other people have a stony heart?" The truth is I don't have a good answer to his question. I don't know why some seem to be on a healthier course than others, or why God's grace radically transforms some people and not others. I don't know why some seed falls on good soil and why other seed falls on rocky ground or among the thorns. But I do know that a new day is on its way when only soft hearts remain.

Our lives all have a direction. Our life is either an accident, or it isn't. We either exist to experience the glory of God, or we do not. I say we do. The deep longings of our heart tell us as much.

You see, behind Pwe Thein's question is something we all feel—a deep longing for a better world. I believe God's new world is coming. Our job is to prepare—to commit to the transformation of our heart. It's not something we do ourselves, but something God does in us. We mustn't cultivate willfulness but *willingness*. "Here I am" becomes the cry of our heart. "Make my heart soft."

If we make becoming a soft-hearted disciple of Jesus Christ our primary aim, our lives will be incredibly rich, meaningful, and eternal, and everything else will fall into place. "Seek first the Kingdom of God," Jesus taught, "and the other things will be added."

It will always be true that even the most committed disciples of Jesus remain clumsy, awkward, and stony, which is why we need a Rescuer in the first place. But we glory in the confidence that we have such a Savior. The God who rolled the stone away that first Easter morning still moves stones. God still moves stones of shame, anger, pride, and contempt. Through the power of Jesus' resurrection, the Spirit of God brings order out of the chaos of our lives. God still clothes His people and prepares them for the Feast.

For what lies beneath our stony heart is a soft heart of flesh. It is only in growing into *this* heart—what St. Paul called the "full stature of Christ"—that we will finally feel "at home." With God. With our world. With our selves. "Here I am."

Discussion Questions

1. Where do you most frequently see "stony hearts" on display in our world? What about in your own life?

2. When did you first sense our world is "out of joint?" How often are you present to a desire for "something more"?

3. Do you think that whatever we place at the center of our life will be the very thing that "forms" us? Why or why not?

4. Is there a difference between the idea of "going to heaven when we die" and the "resurrection of the dead?"

5. How can we "anticipate" God's new world? Is there a difference between cultivating "willfulness" and "willingness?" If so, what is the difference and why is it important?

6. What does the word "sanctification" mean to you? Is our sanctification primarily God's work or our work?

7. How can "faith and hope" remain in God's new world when there's nothing left that's "wrong" or in need of fixing?

CHAPTER 5

Rebirth

I recently officiated at a casual wedding outdoors. Seconds before the ceremony began, a little kid snuck up to me and, tugging on my pant leg, asked me a question.

"What's the deal with the costume?" My clerical collar clearly intrigued this young man. I informed him that I was a priest. "That's awesome!" he said. "Let me see your best magic trick!" This young man had not yet been schooled on the subtle differences between the priesthood and wizardry. "No, I'm a *minister*. I'm the one that gets to marry them." "Ohhhh, so you're the *I do* guy?" And then, seeing my youthful visage, he began to vomit question after question as he processed his epiphany. "Wait! Aren't you way too young to be an *I do* guy? How old are you? How much do you charge? Have you always wanted to be an *I do* guy?" Then he asked the only question that genuinely irritated me. "Are you a professional?"

I'm fine being an "I do" guy. Being mistaken for a wizard is not my favorite, but I've got thick skin. But a *professional*? Is *that* really what I am?

Of course, this is the same question we've been asking all along. What is my *identity? Who am I?* And is anyone a "professional" when it comes to dealing with God?

The Gospel According to John tells a wonderful story about Jesus' encounter with a guy named Nicodemus, who was considered a religious professional by his contemporaries. Nicodemus was a Pharisee, which was a particular "sect" of Judaism. Pharisees focused on right religious rule keeping. We can safely assume that Nicodemus was a respected teacher and that he knew all the right religious rules one had to follow to be considered righteous. People considered him a credentialed expert. People viewed Nicodemus as competent, well qualified, and completely in control of his "religious life."

Yet one can't help but wonder if a completely different story was being played out in Nicodemus' heart of hearts. Like Pwe Thein, I imagine that Nicodemus also longed for a better world. Nicodemus—the credentialed expert, the religious professional, and the one people all depended on to know God—was empty on the inside. So according to St. John he decided to take a shot in the dark—literally. He approaches Jesus at night when no one else is around. Nicodemus has heard that an unconventional, miracle-working rabbi named Jesus teaches about a *different way* of finding worth before God and so Nicodemus decides to hear this "good news" for himself.

> **Nicodemus:** Teacher, we know that God has sent you. Otherwise you would not be able to perform all of these signs.
>
> **Jesus:** In truth I tell you that only people who are born again can see God's kingdom.
>
> **Nicodemus:** How can someone be born a second time? You're not suggesting that someone can enter the womb a second time, *are you*?
>
> **Jesus:** Again, in truth I say that if someone is to enter the Kingdom of God, it will require a new birth by water and by spirit. Don't be so amazed that I'm

teaching that a second birth from above must take place in your life. The Spirit is like the wind and the wind blows wherever it chooses. It's the same with people "born again" by the Spirit.[1]

Jesus' words would have shocked a religious professional like Nicodemus for a million different reasons. Aside from the physical impossibility of a grown man entering his mother's womb a second time for a "do over," for people like Nicodemus it was one's *first birth* that meant everything. For Jews in Jesus' day, being born a legitimate child of Abraham was everything. One's identity was rooted in being "fully" Jewish. One's first birth, quite literally a "birth by water," afforded one the status of "worthy" before God. But a second birth "by spirit"? "How can someone be born a second time?"

As a newly ordained priest, I once referenced our need to be "born again" from the pulpit. A kind woman pulled me aside after the service. She explained that being born again was for *other* denominations and for people in prison, but not for Episcopalians. I found her words ironic because we happened to have had a baptism that day. I realized that we are just as scandalized, confused, and undone by Jesus' teaching here as Nicodemus was.

Telling people they're not fine "as is" simply isn't kosher in today's world. The idea that we have to be "born again," that God must initiate a completely new work in our lives, that we are *not* in control and that we completely lack the resources to save ourselves is a hard pill to swallow. That's why Jesus' teaching on this matter really is controversial. Our spirit is driven to love all the wrong things. Only when God's Spirit intervenes in our lives and softens our heart will the destructive cycle of sin and shame be broken.

---

1 This is my paraphrase of Jn 3:1–8.

After all, we all bind or connect our hearts to something, hoping against hope it can deliver the goods. It is *that something*, whether it be our intelligence or our job or our social status or our looks or what we achieve or our ability to please others, that is the "something" that becomes our functional lord and savior. It becomes the thing *we* rely on to give us significance and worth. We all use something to cover our nakedness and shame. Nicodemus assumed that his first birth and perhaps his vast knowledge of God's law were his "keys to the Kingdom." Election and tradition, it seems, were Nicodemus' loincloths.

But Nicodemus wasn't happy, satisfied, or spiritually fulfilled. Otherwise, he *never* would have sought out Jesus, a rabbi who with only a few words unleashed a wrecking ball that demolished his entire religious worldview.

Nicodemus, listen to me. You must be born from above. What needs to happen in your life is so dramatic that only the metaphor of being born all over again will fit. The Spirit of God is on the move and the Kingdom of God has been thrown open to all, and there isn't a family or tribe or organization in the world that can contain, master, or fully comprehend it. You are NOT the one in control Nicodemus! You see, God's Spirit is just like the wind, and the wind blows where IT chooses, not where you choose. And unless God's Spirit blows your world apart and gives you a completely new identity, a significance and worth based not on your first birth but on this second birth from above, you will never see the Kingdom of God. Do you hear me, Nicodemus? You cannot master God. You must let God master you. No one is a professional in the Kingdom of God.[2]

Our Need Be "Born Again"

We cannot ignore how frequently the Bible references or assumes our desperate need for spiritual rebirth and regeneration. In fact, Jesus' teaching on the new birth did not mark a break from Old Testament teaching and prophesy. Otherwise Jesus would not have chided Nicodemus for not understanding His teaching. "Are you a teacher of Israel," Jesus asked, "and yet you do not understand these things?" (Jn 3:10). In explaining to Nicodemus that he needed rebirth by "water" and by "spirit," Jesus was referencing Ezekiel's prophecy of long ago.

> I will sprinkle clean water upon you, and you shall be clean from all your uncleanness, and from all your idols I will cleanse you. A new heart I will give you, and a new spirit I will put within you; and I will remove from your body the heart of stone and give you a heart of flesh. I will put my spirit within you, and make you follow my statutes and be careful to observe my ordinances. (Ezek 36:25–27)

The New Testament flat out assumes—indeed Christianity is incomprehensible apart from an understanding—that this "new spirit" is at work in those who put on the new clothes Jesus offers by surrendering their lives to God. Jesus tells Nicodemus, "What is born of the flesh is flesh, and what is born of the Spirit is spirit" (Jn 3:6). By virtue of our first birth we are only flesh. "Fleshiness" is our natural human condition. And, as we saw in chapter 2, it is a condition of spiritual enslavement and addiction.

---

2 This is what I would have said to Nicodemus!

This may sound harsh to ears fashioned by a sentimental world of Hallmark cheese, but from the perspective of the Gospel we are spiritually stillborn creatures. Our heart, by nature, is stony. We need an infusion of fresh spiritual life, or what the prophets called a new heart. As Thomas Merton puts it, "As long as I am no longer anybody else than the thing that was born of my mother, I am so far short of being the person I ought to be that I might as well not exist at all."[3] What we need, and what the Gospel offers, is a new birth by "water and by spirit."

Jesus spoke of our need for spiritual rebirth in a million different ways. One of Jesus' favorite images, similar to the image He offered Nicodemus, was that of becoming a child all over again. "Truly I tell you," Jesus said, "unless you change and become like children, you will never enter the kingdom of heaven" (Mt 18:3). Jesus understood that until a Spirit-driven change happens in our heart, we will remain deaf to His message and that the lines of communication between God and ourselves will remain blocked. This is why Jesus ended many of His teachings with, "Let anyone with *ears to hear* listen!" (Mk 4:23, italics mine). The Spirit gives us spiritual ears and eyes to perceive spiritual things.

Spiritual rebirth is ultimately about the restoration of the intimacy with God that we lost in Eden. We recall that Adam and God shared what the Church Fathers called *parrhesia,* which means speech that is free, bold, and sincere. What an amazing thought that Adam and God were best friends! There was no pretense or hiding in their constant conversations. Adam was naked before God and not ashamed at all and every word God spoke was a delight to Adam's ears.

---

3 Thomas Merton, *New Seeds of Contemplation* (New York: New Directions Publishing Corp., 1961), 34.

The tragedy of life in this world is that we inherit not the world God created us for but the banished world of Genesis 4. *Parrhesia* with God no longer comes naturally to we who have stony hearts. Only a spiritual rebirth will soften us and reopen the lines of intimacy and communication. That is why the surest sign that the Spirit is at work in our lives is that we routinely communicate with God. We pray. We listen. We talk to God about the things we are doing together. We take a nightly walk with our Loving Creator in the cool of the day.

How Communication Happens

If spiritual rebirth is about reopening the lines of communication between God and us, and about the restoration of the *parrhesia* that was lost in Eden, it may be helpful to look at how communication works between persons. Communication is more of an emotional phenomenon than an intellectual one. We see this with the parent always trying to "talk sense" into their teen or with the wife who never seems to "get through" to her husband. "Getting through" is an emotional matter of the heart and not a cerebral matter of the brain.

In fact, successfully transmitting a message to another person depends on three things: direction, distance, and anxiety.[4] First, it doesn't matter how eloquently we package our message (or how eloquently God speaks to us) if people's hearts are not directed towards us. Never in the history of the world has someone's heart been melted or someone's mind been converted as the result of an all-out screaming match or by coercive, passive-aggressive jabs. These strategies may use shame to modify someone's behavior in the short run, but they never change hearts or behavior in the long run. The heart direction of *both* persons matters if authentic communication is to

---

4 Edwin Friedman, *A Failure of Nerve* (New York: Seabury, 2007), 128.

take place. Communication happens only when two hearts are attracted and attuned to one another.

Second, distance matters greatly when it comes to someone's capacity to hear us. If I scream as loud as I can, perhaps someone three houses over may hear me but someone three states over will not. The same holds true with distance at the emotional level. This is why the first few years of marriage are so crucial. Problems often surface ten years into a marriage and the couple can't cope because emotionally speaking they have drifted three states over. They never developed the tools to actually listen and communicate with one another. Distance matters. We communicate most freely with people we are emotionally close to and with whom we have earned the right to speak.

Third, anxiety is the most frequently overlooked variable in terms of effective communication. Anxiety is like static. If you've ever listened to a football game on the radio, you'll know that nothing is more frustrating than static. You cannot turn up the volume and dial down the static at the same time. You "miss out on the game."

From time to time an issue will come up in my relationship with Emily that we need to address. She always makes fun of me because I say, "Great. Let's talk about that next Wednesday afternoon." "Can't we talk about it now?" "No. Wednesday afternoon. Final offer."

I think women are genuinely better at "addressing issues" than men. But I know myself far too well. To get a clear, low-static reception I need to talk to Emily Wednesday afternoon when my anxiety has dissipated. Anxiety is a communication killer. There is always an inverse relationship between the level of anxiety between two people and their ability to effectively "get through" to one another. If we are to hear and be heard, the static we call anxiety must be eliminated (or at least toned down).

What Does God Have to Do with It?

What does any of this have to do with spiritual rebirth and returning to God's nudist colony called Eden? The Bible cites three main *parrhesia* inhibitors. In other words, direction, distance, and anxiety keep us barred from Eden.

Directionally speaking, we are *all* running away from God. Humanity has rebelled against the Creator. Like the prodigal son we left our Father's house and we ventured off into the far country. Like Adam we were banished from the garden and have been wandering west ever since. We live in this world allergic to God, "for the inclination of the human heart is evil from youth" (Gen 8:21). What happens when we are spiritually reborn is that what attracts our hearts, or our spirit-drive, begins to change.

Each one of us is "religious." We all bind or connect our hearts to something that attracts us. Spiritual rebirth happens when what we desire more than anything is to know and obey the God and Father of Jesus Christ. Biblical Christianity knows nothing of dry, dutiful religious service. We are born again to "*delight* in the law of the Lord" (Ps 1:2, italics mine). The Bible doesn't invite us to understand and obey, but rather to "taste and see that the Lord is good" (Ps 34:8). If we are to authentically communicate with God, the direction of our hearts must change. We must turn around, come to our senses, and truly desire to run with all of our might into the loving arms of our heavenly Father so that we might enjoy the banquet He has prepared.

The distance between us and God must also be reduced to nil if the lines of communication are to be reopened. Jesus' death on the cross abolished the distance our sins created between us and God. When Jesus breathed his last breath, "the curtain of the temple was torn in two, from top to bottom" (Mk 15:38). That curtain, which was the symbolic separator between God and humanity, has been ripped to shreds by the sacrificial death of Jesus. Jesus bridged the gap between God and humanity by dying for us on the cross. Rather than this being something that God did grudgingly, "God was *pleased* to reconcile to himself all things, whether on earth or in heaven, by making peace through the blood of his cross" (Col 1:20, italics mine). In Christ, God has come *very near*. Jesus says of Himself and His Father, "We will come to them and make our home with them" (Jn 14:23). To be spiritually reborn is to enter a new reality where God is closer to us than we are to ourselves. The distance between God and ourselves has been eliminated.

Finally, God eliminates the anxiety between humanity and our Creator. This is the same anxiety that led Adam and Eve to run away in shame because they knew they were naked and no longer worthy to stand before God. Anxiety, coupled with shame, is why we cover ourselves up with cheap loincloths in the first place. We don't know who we are and so we anxiously try and "make a name for ourselves" (Gen 11:4).

The truth is we are all a bit uneasy with life in this world. We are terrified of the possibility that we are alone and that God does not exist. We are even more terrified of the possibility that God does. As David Elkins puts it, "Existential angst permeates our society. It is in our art, music, literature, movies, and plays: it is behind the increasing rates of anxiety, depression, and suicide; it is the ennui and the sense of hopelessness that threaten to swallow our children."[5]

The most wonderful aspect of spiritual rebirth is that God diminishes the impact of our existential angst. I don't mean to say that Christians aren't susceptible to fear and depression. However, genuine conversion should remove all abject

---

5 David Elkins, *Beyond Religion: A Personal Program for Building a Spiritual Life Outside the Walls of Traditional Religion* (Wheaton, IL: Quest Books, 1998), 62.

hopelessness from our lives once and for all. This does *not* mean God takes away our pain. Jesus' cross will take each one of us up before we can ever take it up and, if anything, Christians will weep *more* (even as they paradoxically also weep less) than they did before encountering God in the first place. But utter despair *is* removed once and for all.

Such is why spiritual rebirth is not about knowing that we are merely forgiven by God. Spiritual rebirth is about knowing that we are cherished and celebrated by God. A radical shift has taken place in our "status" before God. Before our rebirth we dared not approach God naked. In God's own words, "You cannot see my face; for no one shall see me and live" (Ex 33:20). But now we approach God boldly and with confidence. "Let us therefore approach the throne of grace with boldness, so that we may receive mercy and find grace to help in time of need" (Heb 4:16). We have no need to be anxious or ashamed. We have a new wardrobe and have RSVP'd yes to the King's feast. The lines of communication have been reopened. The static has been removed. God has eliminated the existential anxiety between God and us once and for all.

The Objections

It is entirely true that God deals with each person in his or her particularities, idiosyncrasies, and differences. This is how things work between mature persons and we shouldn't expect God to behave any differently. However, there still exists a consistent Gospel message that comes with our spiritual rebirth. The means through which God reaches us with His message may differ. The manner in which we live out God's message will vary from person to person. But the message itself is always the same. "Jesus Christ is the Way, the Truth, and the Life." Jesus Christ is the One we look to for new clothes. Only in Him do we find our worth and true identity. Only Jesus can set us free.

We are reborn to love and serve, and to be loved and served by, Jesus—the very One who was pleased to reconcile all things to Himself.

Before we can take a bite out of the Christian claim that Jesus Christ is the Truth, we first need to chew on the two objections to this claim that are most commonly raised.

Objection #1: It is closed-minded to say that we only know God through Jesus

On the surface this may sound sharp, but upon careful examination we will find that it lacks claws. There is either a Creator or else there isn't. If there is not a Creator, or some other logic (logos) behind the universe, we are all an accident and there is no *why*. And at the end of the day that's that. If there is no God, it matters little where we find our identity or search for meaning in life, whether that be our job, our spouse, some religious system we adhere to, or something else. If we are an accident, then there is no meaning. There is nothing "to know" or be saved from in the first place. Guilt and good works are equally pointless. We will die. Our bodies will dissolve. The earth will be consumed by the sun, which itself will implode millions of years down the road. Christians, Muslims, Moonies, and secularists alike will all be forgotten. In the end Macbeth will be vindicated, though neither he nor his sympathizers will be around to know it. "Life is a tale told by an idiot, full of sound and fury signifying nothing."[6]

When people say that traditional Christian claims are narrow and closed-minded, they are speaking from an emotional place and not an intellectual one. They are unwittingly drawing from the reservoir of the Church's past sins—the Inquisition, the Salem witch trials, and the Church's poor record on slavery and

---

6 This is from one of the most famous soliloquies in Shakespeare's tragedy *Macbeth*. It takes place in the beginning of the fifth scene of Act 5.

civil rights, to name just a few. After all, the Church's reservoir of failings is massive. However, the Church's faithlessness and the truth of Jesus' claims to be Truth itself are two different matters altogether. I am concerned with only the latter of the two. It is quite possible to argue that the traditional claims of Christianity are wrong. But to say that the claims of Christianity *are closed-minded and narrow* is lazy and unjustifiable.

Objection #2: Truth is relative.
The notion of absolute truth is outdated.

Jesus' claim to be "the Truth" is one that many in our world stumble over. Many earnestly believe that truth must be relativized if people are to experience freedom and that all claims to *the* truth, as opposed to "a" truth, are doomed to end in violence. Again, this objection may seduce us on the surface, but in reality it is incomprehensible.

This is also an emotional objection rather than a strong intellectual one. It is hard to underestimate how deep seated our prejudice against absolute truth runs. As Supreme Court Justice Anthony Kennedy once put it, "The heart of liberty is the right to define one's own concept of existence."[7] Relativism is in our western DNA. We are free, or so it is believed, to the extent that we can decide what is true for ourselves.

Two philosophers in particular had a heavy hand in shaping our culture's understanding of truth—Friedrich Nietzsche and Michel Foucault. Their basic message can be summarized: "All truth claims are power plays. When people claim to have the truth, their real motive is to gain power over others and control their behavior."[8] I do not wholly disagree with these two secular prophets. Jesus had the same beef with the Pharisees. The

---

7 http://en.wikiquote.org/wiki/Anthony_Kennedy (accessed 10/3/13)
8 I must confess that my knowledge of these two philosophers is limited and second hand.
I appreciate Peter Rollin's take on Nietzsche in *The Fidelity of Betrayal: Towards a Church Beyond Belief* (Brewster, MA: Paulist Press, 2008), 98–104.

Pharisees were obsessed with "God's truth" and about who was in line with "the truth" and who wasn't. The gospels are littered with Jesus' critique of this particular religious group. When the Church is at her worst she has much more in common with the Pharisees than with Jesus. In fact, all of the Church's sins are the byproduct of being zealously committed to a lie. Nietzsche and Foucault (and Jesus) were correct in saying that when people zealously take a stand for "the truth," there is usually a power play lurking in the background. However, there is a big difference between zealously taking a stand for the truth and humbly living in accordance with the truth, cost what it will. The former places you on the throne and the latter on the cross. Just think of the people we most admire. They are no doubt people who lost their life for the truth.

There is a reason I believe the "truth is all relative" argument is misguided. We all make claims we believe are absolutely true and should be absolutely true for everyone. Nietzsche and Foucault most certainly did. They didn't say that truth claims were sometimes a power play; they said that truth claims were *always* a power play. Atheists do not say that some of us are a molecular accident, but that all of us are an accident. And let's be honest. To hold as one's "absolute truth" that "all truth is relative" is the ultimate power play of all! It keeps us in the position of always being the deflator but never the deflated, which sounds pretty violent and coercive to me.

Jesus was much more realistic than both Nietzsche and Foucault. Jesus wasn't concerned with whether or not we made truth claims. Jesus knew all too well that each one of us would. Jesus' concern was with *who or what* we held as the primary truth that would give meaning and direction to our life. Jesus' invitation was always for us to find truth in *Him*. To put this differently, Jesus' question was never "are you a fundamentalist?" but rather "what fundamental" is guiding and governing your life?

Christians believe that there is indeed Logic behind the universe, and that this Logic is none other than God. Furthermore, Christians hold as truth that this God took on flesh and bones in the Person of Jesus Christ, to suffer and die for a world that had forgotten Him "in order that the world might be saved through Him" (Jn 3:17). What makes us violent and enslaved is not having *a* fundamental, but having the *wrong* fundamental. For example, I recall an old Sprite commercial that told me to "obey my thirst." If that's the fundamental that governs and guides my life, I am a slave. Jesus' message is different. "You will know the truth, and the truth will make you free" (Jn 8:32).

It is a humbling thing to remember that the first Christians were persecuted by a relativistic society where each person was permitted to worship his own god, as long as he was willing to burn incense to Caesar. Behind the "religious tolerance" of the Greco-Roman world was the head of an empire that enslaved his subjects.

What makes Christianity unique is not our belief in absolute truth. What makes Christianity unique is that we don't believe that truth is fully embodied in a creed or a philosophy or a set of rules, but rather in a Person named Jesus Christ. The great irony of our faith is that Jesus' zeal for truth led not to someone else's death but to His own.

Deep down we all know that truth matters greatly. In being a champion for the Civil Rights movement, Martin Luther King, Jr. wasn't a man with fuzzy views on truth, but a systematic theologian (with a Ph.D. from Boston University) who was committed to the truth. In the same way, if a child puts on a superman uniform and stands on the ledge of a ten-story building, it matters greatly whether or not he believes that gravity is true. Gravity exists. We can build a life around its reality or we can ignore its reality, but the truth of gravity is not predicated on our acceptance or rejection of it. Let us not foolishly remark that we are freer if left to decide for ourselves whether or not gravity is true. If the child in the superman costume knows the truth of gravity's existence, the knowledge of that truth will set him free. It's kind of like that with Jesus.

Reborn as "True, Authentic Selves"

Truth matters greatly. Our notion of what is true and real and lasting will shape who or what we bind our hearts to as we search for meaning and worth. To say that Jesus is the Truth is to also say that He alone can reveal our "true identity." Only Jesus can show us the essence of our "true selves." He alone can dress us in new clothes.

This new identity is not something we earn. It always comes as a gift through spiritual rebirth, which happens when we joyfully put our faith in Jesus Christ. By "faith" I don't mean "accepting" Jesus. Faith is about building our emotional and spiritual life around Jesus. Faith is about a lifelong journey of learning from Jesus who we really are.

We are so desperate to know who we truly are. Much of the pathos of human life is tied to the fact that at present we do not have a firm identity to stand on. It shouldn't surprise us to learn that Jesus is eager to answer the identity question for us. However, before we look at what Jesus says about our new identity in Him, it might prove beneficial to unmask a few of the lies we have inherited.

Romanticism, Existentialism, Emotivism, and Identity

Three movements have been especially influential in shaping how we understand ourselves in today's world.[9] The first of these move-

9 I owe my understanding of these three movements (romanticism, existentialism, and emotivism) to N. T. Wright's *After You Believe: Why Christian Character Matters* (New York: HarperCollins, 2010), 50.

ments is Romanticism, a nineteenth century movement that reacted against a cold, "do your duty," rule-based society. Romanticism is all about "inner feeling" and the spontaneous actions that flow when a person is filled with life, love, puppy dogs, and warmth.

Existentialism is the early twentieth century movement that stresses the importance of inner "authenticity," which is still a big buzzword in today's world. "Authentic" people look deep within themselves and find their true, authentic inner being. To live in accordance with one's "true self" is the essence of morality according to the Existentialist.

Emotivism is an outgrowth of both Romanticism and Existentialism. With this movement morality is reduced to what we "like and prefer." Whenever we say things like "treating others with dignity is good," what we really mean is, "I happen to *like* treating people with dignity."

I mention these three movements in particular because they add so very much to our confusion in our search for meaning and worth, or for a "self." As a culture we are heirs to all three narratives. It's as if romanticism, existentialism, and emotivism were thrown into a blender and what came out was a Hamlet shake—"to thine own self be true!" But what does it actually mean to be true to one's self? For example, when my duty is to love my wife, but from within arises a feeling of love and warmth for another woman, what am I to do (romanticism)? Or when I look deep within myself and find that part of me is suspicious of people of color, should I be "authentic" to *that* "true" self (existentialism)? How about when I find myself liking gambling and drinking and telling small lies to get ahead (emotivism)? Does that then mean that it's morally okay?

We have been formed in a world that long ago drank this odd cocktail of romanticism, existentialism, and emotivism to the dregs. They have impacted us at a deep subconscious level. They impact our quest to know who "we are" and diminish our ability to live with confidence in this world. As a result, most of us turn to people and things hoping against hope that *they* might be the one to finally tell us who we are. But they can't. So on we run on the treadmill of trying to find ourselves, and by mid-life the cliché crisis and a fair amount of exhaustion begins to set in. We can no longer deny that our quest has been futile. The people and things we have asked to generate life for us all these years abandon us and prove impotent.

Jesus' Critique of These Movements

Jesus critiques all three of these perspectives. The Romantics are against our duty and big on warm feelings of love. Jesus, however, is big on *both*. Of course, Jesus understands that there are plenty of times when dryness of soul is par for the course. However, the spiritual rebirth the Bible speaks about is one where the affections of our heart gradually come to love what God commands (of course, short of death there will *always* be a part of us that rebels against what God loves). Coming to love what God wills is a process, and it is never easy to retrain one's heart. But time and time again the Bible speaks of this necessity. As the late hymn writer John Newton put it, "Our pleasure and our duty, though opposite before; since we have seen His beauty, are joined to part no more."[10]

Existentialists say, "Look for your life and you will find it," but Jesus says, "Lose your life and you will find it." Unlike the existentialists, Jesus taught that the only way to find our "true selves" is by looking for something beyond our "true selves." Jesus did not teach, "blessed are those who hunger and thirst for happiness," but rather "blessed are those who hunger and thirst for *righteousness*" (Mt 5:6, italics mine).

---

10 Newton, John. "Hymn 3," Christian Classics Ethereal Library, http://www.ccel.org/newton/olneyhymns.h3-3.html (accessed 10/3/13). I encountered this stanza from Newton's hymn in Keller's *The Prodigal God*, page 99.

Finally, nothing is more contrary to Jesus' teaching than emotivism. The night before Jesus died on the cross for the sins of the world, the gospels make it clear that Jesus' preference was to save the world in a different manner. Luke tells us that in Jesus' anguish His sweat turned to blood. "Father," Jesus prayed, "If you are willing, remove this cup from me; yet, not my will but yours be done" (Lk 22:42). Jesus finds that his preference runs counter to the will of His Father, and Jesus chooses to submit to His Father's will. The emotivist worldview says that morality is about conforming to what *we like.* Christianity, however, says that discipleship (I am not comfortable with the phrase *Christian morality*) is about conforming our will, desires, behavior, and affections to what *God likes.*

What is fascinating is that all four worldviews (romanticism, existentialism, emotivism, and Jesus' worldview) are concerned with us becoming free, but the approaches are radically different. Eventually we must take responsibility for the path to freedom we embrace. To not choose and merely "go with the flow" is always to cast our vote against Jesus.

Jesus' Alternative

What Jesus has in common with all three of these movements, as well as with every family system, commercial, and government that has ever or will ever exist, is that he also is concerned with our identity. Jesus' mission is to put us in touch with our "true selves." He longs to transform us into people who love what God commands, who find their life by losing it, and who make their life's mission about pleasing God and not themselves. Jesus' approach to authenticity and identity is different than anything our world has ever seen before. And at the heart of Jesus' plan are the words he spoke to Nicodemus.

"You must be born from above. What needs to happen in your life is so dramatic that only the metaphor of being born all over again will fit. You are NOT the one in control! You see, God's Spirit is just like the wind and the wind blows where IT chooses, not where you choose. And unless God's Spirit blows your world apart and gives you a completely new identity, an identity based not on your first birth but on this second birth from above, you will never see the Kingdom of God."

Part I: Spiritual Rebirth, Faith, and Baptism

The first part of Jesus' plan to help us become our true, authentic selves we have already discussed. We must be reborn supernaturally by the initiating power of God's Holy Spirit. Until this happens, nothing else we do will matter. Our good works and bad works alike will be motivated by self-centeredness, fear, and pride. After all, "good works" make great loincloths. They get people liking and respecting us. They give us power and honor. That is why it is the drive of our spirits that must change. What attracts our hearts must change. What we love and live for must change. Spiritual rebirth isn't about a new plan—it's about a new nature.

The way that our new birth publicly and sacramentally takes hold is through baptism. Baptism and faith are both necessary from the perspective of the New Testament. One is not more important than the other, nor can the two even be separated theologically speaking. The rebirth Jesus spoke of was by *water* and by *spirit*.

God always initiates our search for God. We do not repent and then experience grace; we repent *because* we experience grace. Even the desire to serve God is a supernatural gift of grace. God is always the Initiator.

Part II: Seeking "Self" in the Context of Christ

Perhaps the greatest indicator that Christ is working in our life is that we no longer want to live to gratify the desires of our ego—at least not in the deep places of our minds and hearts. What we love and live for changes. We say of Jesus Christ what John the Baptist did: "He must increase, but I must decrease" (Jn 3:30).

This of course is precisely what Jesus taught. To find our lives we must lose our lives. Part II of Jesus' plan has to do with context. Nothing has life, or an identity, outside of a context. The only exception to this rule is God. God alone is Context. The rest of us have to borrow meaning from a context, whether that is from our job, family, morals, belief system, or something else. For example, if someone asks me, "Is it wrong to burn something?"—I have no clue how to answer their question. If they are asking me to burn music onto a CD or burn firewood to stay warm, then the obvious answer is *no*. My answer would differ, however, if that "something" was my house and the person asking was an arsonist. When it comes to our identity, context is everything.

There is no such thing as identity, *per se*. We only have an identity in a context. Jesus taught that the only context where our true selves could be found is in Him and His Gospel. "For those who want to save their life will lose it, and those who lose their lives for *my sake*, and for the sake of *the gospel*, will save it" (Mk 8:35, italics mine). Jesus tells us that the more we relinquish our quest to find our true selves and let Him take over, the more truly ourselves we become. We look not for our "self" but the truth. As we find the Truth (or perhaps are found by it), the Truth begins to set us free. We begin to gain a glimpse of the person God created us to be.

At some point we need to be honest about something. What so many of us call our "true selves" is nothing more than the train wreck of our family system, heredity, environment, commercials, and peers. I'll never forget having a friend tell me, "I'm my own person. Nobody tells me what to think!" The irony of that particular moment was that he was on his sixth Budweiser because a commercial had told him earlier that week that a supermodel would sleep with him if he just cracked open a few more brews. We choose far less of who we are than we like to imagine. Jesus' antidote to our madness is to stop looking for water in the midst of polluted wells and to give up on our quest to "find ourselves" altogether. *Lose your life and you will find it.* "Strive first for the kingdom of God and *his righteousness,* and all these things will be given to you as well" (Mt 6:33, italics mine). As C. S. Lewis puts it, "Look for yourself, and you will find in the long run only hatred, loneliness, despair, rage, ruin, and decay. But look for Christ and you will find Him, and with Him everything else thrown in."[11] Identity is only given in a context. Someone or something must give us "a name." Jesus Christ is the Logic behind our universe. It is in Him and His Gospel that our true selves are to be found. In baptism and through faith we have died. Our true selves are now hidden with Christ in God.

Part III: Love, Righteousness, and the Way Back Home

It is quite remarkable how frequently God gives the people whom he calls into a covenantal relationship with himself a completely new name. For example, Abram was renamed Abraham. Sarai was renamed Sarah. Jacob was renamed Israel. Saul was renamed Paul. Simon was renamed Peter. I could go on. Our God is in the name-changing business.

Of course, in the words of Juliet, "What's in a name?" In the Bible a name is never merely a name but rather a metaphor for one's identity, or one's truest self. God's desire to rename us is

---

11 Lewis, *Mere Christianity*, 227.

another way of speaking of Jesus' plan to give us a new identity that is secure and unshakable. Christ will give his people "a white stone, and on the white stone is written *a new name* that no one knows except the one who receives it" (Rev 2:17, italics mine).

Jesus understands our dilemma even if we do not. Far from being unique and authentic, the vast majority of us live out a script that the world began handing us long before we were born. Jesus understands that we all have been "named." Our world, family, friends, and government "name" us. The market-place names us. Jesus lived and died as one of us to give us a completely new name.

The Biblical word that best captures this renaming reality is *righteousness,* a word that has to do with lovability and accept-ability. The word righteousness has less to do with our char-acter and more to with being "right with" certain people. It can also mean appropriateness. If someone invites me to a black tie affair and I show up in blue jeans and boots, I would sense at a deep, deep level how inappropriate or "unrighteous" that I am. This particular example mirrors Jesus' parable, where the man showed up to the king's party and refused to put on a wedding robe. He was not "right with" his host. To his horror he discov-ered that, as he was, he was utterly inappropriate and that he did not fit in at the king's party.

What does all this have to do with our identity or name? As we discussed in chapter 2, our need for worth, for a name, and for an identity is so powerful that whatever we base our identity on becomes our functional god. It becomes our reli-gion and the thing we bind or connect our heart to. That which we bind or connect our heart to becomes our "righteousness"—the thing we rely on to feel appropriate and loveable in this world.

Now it is not fair to say that the word righteous can always be translated lovability or acceptability. In the Bible the word righteous is always tied to God's covenant and is used to describe both an attribute of God as well as something that humanity strives for. Whenever the word righteousness is used of God it means "covenant faithfulness." To say that God is righteous is to say that God will fulfill His end of the promise to bring his wayward image-bearers back to Eden and reconcile all things to Himself.

But on the other side of this theological coin we find that our spirits are driven by an unconscious quest to return to Eden. Just as God's righteousness has to do with God's promise to offer us a Way back to Eden, our quest for righteousness has to do with the many ways we try and return to the peace, stability, and harmony that God created us for. We do this in a million different ways. We commit ourselves to some self-salvation project that we think will bring us home. However, it is only through Christ and His atoning work on the cross that we are given the appropriate garment that enables us to come back home to the Feast.

Faith

Spiritual rebirth is about putting our faith in Jesus Christ. It is about being renamed and receiving new clothes. Faith isn't so much a matter of weighing the evidence and accepting or rejecting certain doctrinal truths about Jesus, though the use of our reasoning faculties is always present and even perfected as we grow in grace. But faith is about learning to trust in a Living Person. It is about changing our mind about whom or what we want to bind our heart to in order to derive a sense of self. That's why it's a false statement when people say, "I'd like to believe but faith is hard!" Faith isn't hard. Faith is actually the most natural thing in the world. When it comes to faith we all have it. That's why growing into the full stature of Christ isn't so much about calling a faith into existence that previously did not exist. Rather, the challenge of discipleship is to *transfer* our faith—from whatever its focus now is to Jesus Christ, the Logic behind our universe and our lives.

This is a point a lot of people in today's world fail to understand. A false dichotomy exists between faith and reason. "He's a spiritual guy, but I'm much more rational," people say. But that's nonsense. We all put our faith in something. Reason always interprets a faith system, or works within a context. I believe that I was created because God is love and that a real purpose or logic exists behind the universe. Others believe that we are an accidental coming together of atoms and that no grand design exists. Let's not be foolish and call one "spiritual" and the other "rational." *Both* are statements of faith. *Both* are built on systems of belief. Everyone has faith.

We all live by faith. We make decisions every day about what is important and how to treat people and what makes us valuable. These decisions inevitably flow out of our deepest beliefs about the world. When it comes to how we live, it is never a question of faith or no faith, belief or no belief. We are always talking about faith *in what?* Belief in *what?* The question in the Christian life is never whether we have faith or not. The question in the Christian life is always, "What have we put our faith in?" We are *all* fundamentalists. What is *our* fundamental—Jesus, or something else?

On Being a Child

This is not something we can control, yet we *are* responsible for our lives before God. The spiritual rebirth that God offers us in Christ is a gift and it can only be received as such. As Thomas Merton once noted, "It is not we who choose to awaken ourselves, but God Who chooses to awaken us."[12] The change that must take place in our lives is so radical that only the metaphor of being "born again" will work.

---

12 Merton, *New Seeds of Contemplation*, 10.

We must not make the same mistake Nicodemus did and fail to understand Jesus' teaching. Through the cross of Jesus Christ, God has taken away the anxiety and distance that exists between us, and is turning human hearts *towards* Him. In the process, God is offering us a true faith and a new life that comes as we bind our hearts to His Son. Jesus alone is our righteousness. Jesus' worth is our worth and it is His name that secures our new name.

The Kingdom of God is all around us. But do we see it? Are our lives rooted in it? Have we been completely undone by it? According to St. John we need to be "born again." According to St. Matthew we need to change and become like children. According to St. Paul we need a spirit of adoption. We may choose any metaphor we like, because at the end of the day they're all talking about the same thing.

In other words, it's not just that there aren't any professionals in the Kingdom of God. It's that in the Kingdom of God, there aren't any adults.

Discussion Questions

1. Do you believe we need to be "born again"? What does this phrase mean to you?

2. What do you think "successful communication" with God and others depends on? Direction? Distance? Anxiety? What else?

3. Does God remove utter despair from Christians? What about anxiety? What is the difference between despair and anxiety?

4. Jesus claims to be the way, the truth, and the life. What do you think Jesus means by this? What does Jesus *not* mean when He claims to be the Truth?

5. Is it true that we only have an "identity" in a context? Is there a "you" apart from something or someone else?

6. How do other people "name" us? How does Jesus give us a "new name" that frees us?

7. Do you believe all people have faith? Do you think we can always see what we have put *our faith* in?

CHAPTER 6

Rooting and Fruiting

My junior year of high school I spent Labor Day weekend with some friends at the beach on the Texas gulf coast. I ventured off from my group momentarily and was approached by a young man about my age. As he greeted me with his right hand, I noticed the Bible in his left hand. Circumventing any formal introduction, he asked me a question that every person from Southeast Texas is asked at least once by a complete stranger. *Are you saved?*

With all the maturity of a sixteen-year-old, I began to flail around in a sarcastic panic and scream "from what?" The young man was not amused. He pressed on. "If you were to die tonight," he said, "are you certain that you would be with God in heaven?" Not knowing exactly how to respond, I assured him that I was a devout Episcopalian. Knowing exactly how to respond, he assured me that Episcopalians were not saved—*especially* the devout ones.

An awkward silence followed, which the young man eventually broke with words that were poetic and beautiful. He told me about God's love for me and about God's great desire to be in relationship with me. "Salvation," he said is "the key to our existence. Being born again is the opportunity of a lifetime."

But then something changed. He handed me a tract the size of a business card. The card's contents listed three simple steps necessary to being born again. "Take a card," he said, "Salvation is easy."

I am not sure why this memory persists with such force in my psyche. I come back to this memory a lot. I think it's the young man's final statement that gets me—"salvation is easy." It rubs me wrong because while I know in my heart that he is right, I also know from experience he is wrong. How can death and resurrection—a completely new birth by water and spirit— be easy? *Minute Rice* is easy. But being reborn a completely new self in Jesus Christ? Is *easy* the right adjective to describe this grace-initiated and grace-sustained metamorphosis of the soul?

On the one hand, salvation *is* easy in that the Gospel can be simply stated—"Christ died for the ungodly" (Rom 5:6). We are saved not by our works but by Christ's death for us and by His life in us. But on the other hand, living *for* Jesus is anything but easy. Gospel living cannot be confined to a card. In fact, St. Paul says that we cannot even fully grasp the fullness of the Gospel we proclaim (Rom 11:33). The Gospel is not a set of beliefs to master but a Mystery to master us. It's ironic that the call to discipleship is an invitation to know the love of Christ that surpasses knowledge (Eph 3:19). We are spiritually reborn for a purpose. God wants us to grow into the Gospel's mystery and be changed from the inside out.

This beach evangelist was right that we who put our faith in Christ *are* saved. We have received the "new clothes" of salvation, which is nothing less than an unshakable new identity as God's special child and an unassailable sense of worth based on Jesus Christ's record of perfect obedience. Our moral record becomes obsolete as Jesus' record before God becomes ours, too.

And yet, on the other hand, we have not yet arrived in God's new world. We live as new people in the midst of an old world, "for the present form of this world is passing away" (1 Cor 7:31). We live as new selves who are daily assaulted by our old, dead self. We have the new clothes of God's salvation but they don't yet fit. We are God's special children and immature babies all at the same time. A saying often attributed to Martin Luther is that we are *simul iustus et peccator*—"at the same time righteous and a sinner."[1] No one captures this paradox better than Peter, who says: "Like newborn infants, long for the pure, spiritual milk, so that by it you may grow into salvation—if indeed you have tasted that the Lord is good" (1 Pet 2:2–3).

This is the paradox of the Christian life. On the one hand we are saved. "It is finished" (Jn 19:30). We are totally and fully *iustus*—righteous and justified in the eyes of God. We may present ourselves to God as one already approved (2 Tim 2:15). And this remains true even *if* we don't "get better" from whatever loincloths that enslave us.

But on the other hand, Jesus invites us to grow into the salvation we already have as we anticipate the full arrival of God's New World. The garment of salvation we already possess doesn't fit. The garment of salvation I've been given is a 44-long and at present my jacket size is a 36-short. Salvation *is* simple and free and comes as a gift. But we must grow into it. And the growth process, contrary to what my proselytizing Christian brother on the beach told me, is *anything* but easy. And the reason for that is simple: growth in the Christian life looks more like crucifixion than it does "resurrection." And being crucified is far from easy. Jesus has already given us everything. And yet, he longs to take what we vainly imagine is "everything" from us. "Very truly, I tell you, unless a grain of wheat falls into the earth and dies, it remains just a single grain; but *if it dies*, it bears much fruit" (Jn 12:24, italics mine). And this we call "growth."

Growing into Our Salvation

Growing into a salvation that we have already received is sustained in our lives as we say "yes" to God's work of transforming

---

1 http://en.wikipedia.org/wiki/Theology_of_Martin_Luther (accessed 10/4/13)

us from the inside out. We who have been reborn into the family of God through faith and baptism are to seek and pray for the renovation of our heart and the transformation of our character. Who we become in this life, or the "content of our character," is of far more importance than anything we do. God wants us to grow up to have the heart of Jesus Christ. Henry Nouwen writes:

> In our world of loneliness and despair, there is an enormous need for men and women who know the heart of God, a heart that forgives, that cares, that reaches out and wants to heal. In that heart there is no suspicion, no vindication, no resentment, and not a tinge of hatred. It is a heart that wants only to give love and receive love in response.[2]

Nouwen's statement wonderfully summarizes the primary aim of the Christian life—to have our heart conformed to the heart of Jesus Christ so that we can live our lives in this world doing the things that Jesus routinely did with His spirit and humility. "Doing the right things" is not enough. We must do them with the heart of Jesus Christ. Of course the question is always how does this happen? How do stony hearts become soft?

The Lie: We Change Through Willpower

Jesus' vision for how hearts are transformed at first seems a little counterintuitive. Spiritual growth is not something *we* make happen.

Most of us, when we decide to make a change, only have one plan—we roll up our sleeves and we try really, really hard. The problem is that our willpower is actually pretty impotent. I know we learned something different growing up. As long as I can remember, people have said, "You can do *anything* you set

---

2 Henri Nouwen, *In the Name of Jesus* (New York: Crossroad, 1992), 24.

your mind to!" But the Christian Gospel would strongly disagree with such a statement. Our spirits may be willing but our flesh is weak and impotent (Mt 26:41).

Jesus' vision for the spiritual life differs from Nike's vision. We cannot "just do it." We do not grow in the Gospel by exercising our moral muscles. After all, Jesus Christ is not a drill sergeant. Jesus is a surgeon (Mt 9:12). Jesus is a farmer (Lk 8:5). He's a shepherd (Jn 10:11). But Jesus is *not* a drill sergeant that sits on heaven's throne with a megaphone shouting to humanity day after day, "Try harder! You're lazy! Pick it up!"

In the long run "trying harder" to be more Christ-like is a bad strategy. We will most likely fail and feel a deep sense of shame, and upon feeling shame use something unhealthy to medicate our shame, thus falling deeper into sin's destructive spiral. Or worse, we will walk the road of the Pharisee; we will "succeed," and upon succeeding we will feel pride and eventually look down on people that don't quite have it all together like we do. Either path is a major spiritual regression. In the New Testament the Pharisees were on a mission to change everyone. And they were unbearable.

This is how Jesus describes our work in the Gospel According to St. John:

> I am the true vine, and my Father is the vinegrower. He removes every branch in me that bears no fruit. Every branch that bears fruit he prunes to make it bear more fruit. You have already been cleansed by the word that I have spoken to you. Abide in me as I abide in you. Just as the branch cannot bear fruit by itself unless it abides in the vine, neither can you unless you abide in me. (Jn 15:1–4).

In this passage we find the paradox that makes talking about spiritual transformation so hard. And that paradox goes something like this: The transformation of our heart is not something we do, and yet there is something we must do! "My Father is the vinegrower," Jesus said. Our growth is God's work. "Unless you abide," Jesus said, "you will not grow." We must take responsibility for staying close to Jesus so that He can do His proper work in us.

Perhaps the best way to tap into this paradoxical mystery is to make a distinction between bearing fruit and being productive. To quote Nouwen once more:

> In our contemporary society, with its emphasis on accomplishment and success, we often live as if being productive is the same as being fruitful. Productivity gives us a certain notoriety and helps take away our fear of being useless. But if we want to live as followers of Jesus, we must come to know that products, successes, and results often belong more to the house of fear than the house of love.[3]

What Nouwen claims is revolutionary. He suggests that our need to achieve and produce, even in the spiritual life, most often comes not from a place of love or even genuine goodwill, but rather from a place of fear. I must confess that I wholeheartedly agree. A small measure of fear is motivating the writing of this book. "If I don't publish a book, who am I?" Yes, this book is a labor of love. But Jesus also taught that the weeds and wheat couldn't be separated this side of God's New World. This book, in part, is an extension of my desperate need to please, perform, and perfect so that people will love me and the world will clap. Part of me doesn't yet understand that God will applaud no matter what I do or don't do.

---

3 Henri Nouwen, *Lifesigns: Intimacy, Fecundity, and Ecstasy in Christian Perspective* (New York: Doubleday, 1986), 48–49.

I say all this without an ounce of shame because, until God's New World fully dawns, some fear will always motivate even my best actions. As I mentioned earlier, deep down we are all terrified that we have no value and so we try and *produce it.* We excel, we serve, we volunteer, and we people-please. Like the story of Babel in Genesis 11, we build not a tower but a shining image that we take with us into the world. And we say subconsciously what the builders of Babel did: "Let us make a name for ourselves" (Gen 11:4). We do that because we don't fully believe that God has *already* given us a new name.

Being a really good person, serving others, and winning approval is a tried and true way to make a name for ourselves in this world. Some of the best loincloths are distributed at our churches. "Dressing up" as a good Christian can make us feel really secure. But as Nouwen reminds us, freedom comes when we tell the truth about the deep *insecurity* and *fear* that keep us dressing up. There is very little difference between being a prodigal son and an elder brother (Lk 15). Both must swallow their pride and come freely to the feast.

Spiritual growth is not something we do, and yet we all know we have a part to play. To tap into *our* part, we must take as our spiritual foundation what Jesus says in John 15:3—"You have *already* been cleansed" (italics mine). A new, unshakable identity has already been given us through the merits of Jesus' death and resurrection.

This is so important because the first thing we must drop when seeking to grow in the salvation we *already have,* is the idea that we have something to prove or that God will meet us halfway if we only roll up our sleeves and do the rest. Babel is about making a name for ourselves. Baptism is about receiving a new name through the grace of God. In fact, twice in the Bible, God cries out, "It is finished!" The first is in creation on the seventh day (Gen 2:1); the second cry is uttered from the cross (Jn 19:30). The Bible's point is that both creation and redemption belong to God, and as far as God is concerned they are finished! Of course, the drama of salvation has not yet fully played out in our lives or in our world. This is why we must anticipate it. But as St. Paul notes, the God "who began a good work among you will bring it to completion by the day of Jesus Christ" (Phil 1:6). St. Paul's point is foundational: It is finished. We have already been cleansed. We have absolutely nothing to prove.

Such is why spiritual growth happens not when we *do* something but when we *root ourselves* in something that has already been done. We already have the multi-colored coat. Spiritual growth is about growing into it. I know at first such a distinction might seem confusing. But it is absolutely vital if we are to understand how and why we are to grow into the amazing gift of salvation that we have already received.

The Truth—We Change by Indirection

We grow in the grace we have already been given through a process called "indirection." We don't change by *directly* focusing on "trying harder" to be like Jesus. Rather, we change "indirectly" as we focus on spiritual practices that will strengthen our emotional and spiritual muscles by putting us in touch with the truth of who we already are in Christ. At present we simply cannot drop some habits, attitudes, prejudices, and areas of habitual wrongdoing. Like St. Paul we often find ourselves doing the very things we hate over and over again (Rom 7:15). That's why sin is a destructive and shame-filled spiral. We root ourselves in the finished work of Christ to taste and experience and live into the freedom we already have.

We may not be able to shed our patterns of selfishness, defensiveness, irresponsibility, and unbridled consumerism overnight. However, we *can* pray. We can study Scripture. We can volunteer for an hour a week reading to underprivileged kids.

We can do the dishes, rub our wife's back, and turn off the TV to listen to her, not because she needs those things—though she most certainly does—but rather because *we* need to do them. It is *our* selfish grasping ego that must be crucified. It is our heart that God has given us dominion over. It is the chaos of our lives that God longs to bring order to. This is what I mean by "indirection." We focus on what we can do, God adds the secret ingredient of His Spirit, and over time we grow into people that "do the things Jesus did and more" (see Jn 14:12). We may not be able to operate on ourselves. But we can find clever ways to strap ourselves to the table.

Rooting

The meaningful work God created us for isn't found in mustering our willpower and changing the world, but rather in rooting ourselves in Jesus Christ and bearing fruit for God. I once was asked to speak about this to a church and began by saying, "Thank you for having me. Tonight I'd like to talk to you about rooting and fruiting." I immediately regretted that decision.

But then again "rooting and fruiting" best describes the work Jesus has given us to do. Rooting and fruiting is what Jesus meant when he said "abide" in me, a word that means to "actively seek to remain." As we "abide" in Jesus, our life becomes a joy-filled endeavor of rooting ourselves deeper and deeper in Jesus Christ so that our lives bear fruit.

The Necessity of Joy

It would be misleading to say that this is something we "have" to do. Spiritual growth isn't a duty but an ever-growing life of freedom. Biblical Christianity doesn't endorse dry, religious observance, nor can Jesus' message be reduced to a firm admonition to "do your duty." Jesus came to offer us abundant life and unimaginable joy. A continual willingness to root our lives in Jesus is the only thing that will unlock the joy that He offers us. Obedience and joy always go together.

God's invitation to root and bear the fruit of a changed life is all over the Bible. "You will know them by their fruits," Jesus said. "A good tree cannot bear bad fruit, nor can a bad tree bear good fruit" (see Mt 7:15–20). St. Paul says the *fruit* of the Spirit is "love, joy, peace, patience, kindness, generosity, faithfulness, gentleness, and self-control" (Gal 5:22–23). And in St. John's Gospel, Jesus says plainly, "My Father is glorified by this, that you bear much fruit and become my disciples" (Jn 15:8). But perhaps my favorite Biblical image of the rooting and fruiting joy-filled life is found in Psalm 1:

> Happy are those who do not follow the advice of the wicked, or take the path that sinners tread, or sit in the seat of scoffers; but their delight is in the law of the Lord, and on his law they meditate day and night. They are like trees planted by streams of water, which yield their fruit in its season, and their leaves do not wither. In all that they do, they prosper. (Ps 1:1–3)

It should be clear from Psalm 1 that a life of obedience to Jesus is, ironically, in our own best interest. "Happy" are those who follow the right path, we are told. "Their delight is in God's law." This perfectly aligns with what Jesus said his purpose was in calling us to obey Him—"So that my joy may be in you, and that your joy may be complete" (Jn 15:11). Obedience and joy go hand in hand.

This image of Christian faithfulness is not what many of us were taught in Sunday school. The righteous person, we always assumed, would be more like an activist or a champion or a go-getter or a goodie-two-shoes. But Psalm 1 paints a much different picture. The righteous person is like a *tree*.

What Kind of Tree Are We?

I will never forget the day this image sank in.[4] A tree goes through changing seasons. It must endure winter and times of famine and even the occasional forest fire. This implies something all mature Christians already know to be true. The fruit of authentic faith is not superficial happiness or a life that is free from pain or loss. The tree in Psalm 1 does not bear fruit in *all* seasons. It bears fruit in "its" season. Not all seasons does it bear fruit but "some" seasons.

What makes this tree different from other trees therefore has nothing to do with what happens to it but rather with where it has been planted. The tree of Psalm 1 is planted by a riverbank. The Psalm 1 tree has the capacity to put its roots deep down beneath the surface of the earth. As a result, when the drought comes this tree still has access to streams of living water.

This is the perfect image for a life rooted in Jesus Christ whereby we grow through a gradual process of *indirection*. Metaphorically speaking, there is a big difference between being a tree planted by the river and one that must depend on the outside rain to nourish it. People whose lives are nourished as they draw on the inner resource of an intimate relationship with God are different than people that depend on "outside factors," or what I have called "loincloths," for a sense of self or for an identity. The problem is that we can never control whatever "outside factor" it is we mistakenly believe will generate life for us. We can only violently fight for our share of the pie.

We can liken the size of our bank account, our health, our reputation, how we look and feel, and whether life turns out as we always dreamt it would to the rain. If we depend on any of these loincloths for our sense of meaning and joy, we are toast.

---

4 It was a sermon by Dr. Timothy Keller that made me present to the power of this metaphor.

For we will either get all these things and live a superficial life, or more likely, we will be denied them and become bitter and cynical. The psalmist's point, and the consistent witness of the Bible, is that we cannot depend on any outside factor for our sense of self, meaning, and joy—or what I have called our "identity." Like the tree depicted in Psalm 1 we have to be rooted. We must draw on something that is not subject to changing circumstances. And of course that something is God.

We recall what Jesus said to a Samaritan woman by a well. "Everyone who drinks of this water will be thirsty again, but those who drink of the water that I will give them will never be thirsty" (Jn 4:13–14). Drinking up Jesus' living water is what rooting and fruiting is all about. But we must experience this water for ourselves. The Bible doesn't invite us to think and see. It says we are to "*taste* and see" that the Lord is good (Ps 34:8, italics mine).

The Transformation

A life of rooting and fruiting will increase our capacity to taste the freedom we already have. We will grow into the salvation we have already received. We will come to feel more and more at home in God's Kingdom.

Of course this process of transformation is mysterious, as is any process involving both Divine and human agency. But it would be wrong to label it as incomprehensible. When the grace of God breaks into our lives, there are certain practices, all of which were part of Jesus' life, that if faithfully engaged can reshape our heart. What can we do to plant ourselves by streams of living water? God no doubt has His part (vine-growing, pruning, etc.). However, it is our part (abiding) I will be concerned with from here on out.

I can't claim to be telling the whole truth here, but I do believe that I can offer the basics when it comes to the process of spiritual re-formation. The process might at first seem confusing, both on paper and in reality, because spiritual growth is not linear but circular. In the spiritual life, we do not move from stage A to B to C and so on and so forth up the ladder until we reach our goal. Spiritual growth is not a neat and tidy 12-step process (although certain steps are certainly helpful guideposts!). Rather, A takes us to B and back to C, which always leads us back to A. It's a process that's both exhilarating and crushing (which is God's finest work!). We never end up where we think we will or hope to be. For only God knows what our future transformed glory self looks like. And it is *that* self, not our religious, fully obedient super ego, that God is chomping at the bit to clothe us in.

The Process

Let us now look at the spiritual formation process itself. The transformational pattern whereby we acquire the heart of Jesus Christ has some things in common with other patterns of transformation. For example, let's say your goal wasn't to become more Christ-like but to learn French. The same three things would be required, which many have named the "VIM" pattern. VIM is an acronym for vision, intention, and means—all three of which are necessary for personal transformation of any kind to take place in our lives.

First, we must have a clear *vision* for what transformation looks like and must know in our bones that such a vision is compelling and worth whatever effort or inconveniences may be required of us. Sticking with the language metaphor, perhaps we are moving to Paris; if we don't learn French, then we won't be able to communicate. The vision of speaking French to get by in Paris would totally be worth the effort.

Second, we must truly *intend* to live into our vision. Realizing a vision always involves at least some level of sacrifice. It's one thing to wonder how nice it would be to speak French.

It's another thing to want it so badly that you are willing to set aside an hour each day for the next two years to learn the new language. Lots of people buy Rosetta Stone. Few people learn the language.

Third, you must have adequate *means* at your disposal to live into your vision. Perhaps in this case it is French classes, flash cards, a tutor, and an alarm clock to wake you up an hour earlier each day. But either way, this is the reliable tried and true pattern for change. Three things are always required—vision, intention, and means. Dallas Willard puts it:

> If we are to be spiritually formed in Christ, we must have and must implement the appropriate *vision, intention*, and *means*. Not just any path we take will do. If this VIM pattern is not put in place properly and held there, Christ simply will not be formed in us.[5]

Willard's great gift is to help us understand the mystery of personal transformation just enough to *enter* into it. The three components of vision, intention, and means will always be present in our transformation into Christlikeness. Here is how I speak of each of these components.

> **Vision:** Here we discern what it means for me to live *my* life in *my* context with *my* unique circumstances, gifts, and weaknesses with the heart of Jesus Christ. Our vision for what it means to be obedient to Jesus is always in the process of being reshaped and refined as our circumstances change and our knowledge base grows.
>
> **Intention:** This is about strengthening our resolve to "press on toward the goal" that we set in our vision

---

5 Dallas Willard, *Renovation of the Heart: Putting on the Character of Christ* (Colorado Springs, CO: NavPress, 2002), 85.

(Phil 3:14). After all, Jesus told us to count the cost and to think *seriously* about whether we've got what it takes to see the journey to its end (see Lk 14:25–33).

Means: This is where *indirection* kicks in. We focus on what we can do to strengthen our muscles to learn to accomplish what, at present, we cannot do. Three means are indispensable—prayerful reflection, authentic community, and a commitment to radical obedience.[6]

Remember, this transformational process is not linear but circular. We do not move from V to I to M, but rather from V to I to M and back to V. See Diagram 6-1.

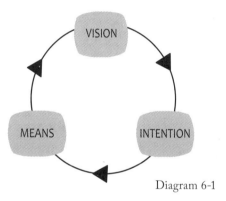

Diagram 6-1

But even that is overly simplistic. For example, three things belong in the *means* column when it comes to our personal transformation. These are prayerful reflection, a commitment to a life of radical obedience to Jesus, and an authentic community of fellow disciples that are in the habit of extending grace and truth to one another. In reality such a process might look much more like Diagram 6-2.

---

6 These three means of "obedience, authentic community, and prayerful reflection" are inspired by a retreat I went on called "Faithwalking." Faithwalking is a ministry of Mission Houston: http://faithwalking.blogspot.com/

Diagram 6-2

Here we find that as a person engages in prayerful reflection, only then does a vision for what is needed for her to grow up spiritually emerge. She then reflects on that vision in the context of an honest and loving community, whose wisdom and encouragement and presence strengthen her intention to practice more obedience to Jesus. As she seeks to obey, she finds new places where she is habitually failing to be faithful and is able to confess those places in her life that she doesn't trust God without an ounce of shame or fear. She can tell the truth about the myriad ways she does not have it all together. Her community extends grace and understanding, for they are pilgrims on the same journey and are honest about their own weakness. She is also able to celebrate with her community the "small wins" she enjoys and the growth that she sees, all of which strengthen her intention to be faithful and drive her even *deeper* into a life of prayerful reflection. This of course strengthens her vision for what it might look like to live with the heart of Christ in whatever unique setting she happens to find herself in.

Maybe circular systems diagrams drive you crazy. I'll offer a more static image, which perhaps is more accessible. Think of a three-legged stool where each of the legs represents one aspect in the "means" column. In this model it is the three legs of prayerful reflection, authentic community, and radical obedience that hold up a life whereby we are always clarifying our vision and strengthening our intention to realize it. See Diagram 6-3.

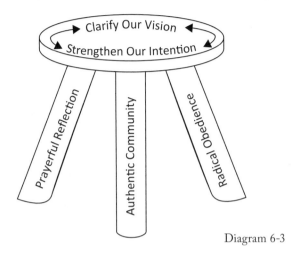

Diagram 6-3

Jumping into the Process

This is where things get even messier. I would like to begin with *prayerful reflection*, which is only one aspect of the "means" column. You might be wondering, "Why not start with vision?" Apart from at least some form of prayerful reflection, our vision for what it means to live in this world with Jesus' heart will be woefully off base and egocentric. In the spiritual life we *always* start with prayer.

Consider Peter's mistake in Matthew 16: If you had asked Peter to begin with *his vision,* his reply would have been to build an army, slit the throats of the Romans, restore the political dynasty of Israel, and serve as Jesus' chief of staff. Peter's vision was way off base. When Jesus first predicted that he would be crucified, Peter rebelled. "God forbid it, Lord! This must never happen to you" (Mt 16:22). Peter's problem was that he had a very clear vision of what it meant to follow Jesus, and His vision could not have been more wrong!

In my experience, each one of us is like Peter. Our initial vision for what a life of obedience and abundance in Jesus' Kingdom looks like should not be trusted. Rather, our vision must emerge out of a life of prayerful reflection and continually be sharpened in the context of an authentic community. Think of Jesus. He did not begin his ministry with a vision but in prayer. According to Luke, when Jesus was baptized by John, he "was praying" (Luke 3:21). In preparation for choosing the twelve, he went up the mountain alone and "spent the night in prayer" (Luke 6:12). Mark tells us that after an exhausting night of healing "many who were sick" and "casting out many demons," Jesus got up early in the morning "while it was still very dark . . . and went out to a deserted place, and there he prayed" (Mark 1: 34-35). It was Jesus' prayer life that led him to a vision whereby He would save the world by dying for it.

Or perhaps we can put this in medical terms. Every doctor worth his salt knows that the most vital aspect of the treatment process is not the prescription. It is the diagnosis. Without an accurate diagnosis the "vision for moving forward" simply won't work. When we look at the etymology of this word, we begin to see how important an accurate diagnosis is. The word derives from two Greek words, *gnosis* and *dia*. The word *gnosis* means "knowledge" and *dia* means "through and through."[7] The word diagnosis means to know someone or something through and through.

Prayerful reflection is where we obtain an accurate diagnosis. The point is to come to know God and ourselves through and through. Peter had the wrong treatment plan (kill the Romans) because he failed to grasp the real problem (sin and death). Peter misdiagnosed the situation. This is why we cannot begin with vision and why the process of our growth into Christlikeness is not linear. Any good carpenter knows that it is best to "measure twice, cut once." That is why we begin with prayerful reflection. It is how we ensure that our vision is worth pursuing.

---

7 I derive this point from Henri Nouwen's *Reaching Out: The Three Movements of the Spiritual Life* (New York: Doubleday, 1975), 95.

Prayerful Reflection

Prayerful reflection is a complex reality. Many books have been written on this subject, including two of my favorites: Richard Foster's *The Celebration of Discipline* and Dallas Willard's *The Spirit of the Disciplines*. I deem three components to be most crucial—prayer, Scripture, and self-examination.

Prayer

Prayer is about walking humbly with our God in a posture of mutual dialogue. It is about putting before God what concerns us and speaking candidly with God about what we are doing *together* in His world. It's about listening to what God has to say in response. Prayer is the language of God's New World.

St. Augustine once said, "Our hearts are restless, O Lord, until they rest in thee." His point was that we *all* long for God at a deep, deep level. Prayer begins with the realization that God *also* longs for us, in fact far more so than we could ever long for Him. Richard Foster says:

> Today the heart of God is an open wound of love. He aches over our distance and preoccupation. He mourns that we do not draw near to him. He grieves that we have forgotten him. He weeps over our obsession with muchness and manyness. He longs for our presence.[8]

It is an amazing thing to consider that the God of the universe longs for our presence. Sadly, far too many of us think we need to fine-tune our lives and sort through our motives before we can begin praying. But this idea arises from a misunderstanding of both prayer and the nature of God. C. S. Lewis once remarked that in prayer we don't lay before God what we *think* ought to be in us, but what actually is in us. To pray authentically, we

---

8 Richard Foster, *Prayer: Finding the Heart's True Home* (New York: HarperCollins, 1992), 7.

must believe that God is good. After all, we all carry within us so much darkness, pain, mixed motives, and foolish desires. In the Episcopal Church we pray, O God, "you know our necessities before we ask, and our ignorance in asking."[9] If we were to wait until our motives were pure before we began praying, it is certain that we would never get started.

That is why it might not be healthy to pray for world peace when all you can think of is how worried you are about your children or even how disappointed you are in God. God is not well served when we speak to Him about one thing while our heart is focused on something else. Consider the prayer of the Jewish man in exile that prays for the violent death of the Babylonian babies (Ps 137:9), or the man with no hope in an afterlife that asks God to leave Him alone so that he can die in peace (Ps 39:13). These men's emotional states by no means reflect God's heart. And yet, darkness and pain were their reality and they trusted God enough to offer it up to Him in prayer. *In prayer we lay before God not what we think should be in us, but what in fact actually is in us.* And we do so because God is *good.* God wants us to know that being honest with God is safe and that it fosters intimacy. Plus, it's not like God doesn't already know!

Of course in prayer we do not just pray for ourselves, but for others as well. Traditionally this is called *intercession,* which has to do with longing for what is best for someone before God. Intercessory prayer is a way of loving people and serving them. This is why to intercede for someone, we need to know their needs, their flaws, and their strengths. I truly believe that intercession changes things and circumstances, for otherwise it would be a psychologically impossible exercise. But more importantly, intercessory prayer changes *us.*

If there is someone in your life who has been driving you crazy, or that you complain about on a daily basis, I can say for

---

9 The Collect for Proper 11, *The Book of Common Prayer,* 231.

certain that you have *not* been interceding for them. You have not been praising God for their strengths, which would require taking the time to name them. Nor have you been humbly asking God to work on their flaws and to show you your part in the problem. You've just been whining. I know this because the act of thoughtfully and carefully interceding for someone always softens our heart towards that person. It is why Jesus told us to pray for our enemies (Mt 5:44). Interceding for them helps us see first and foremost that they are our enemies, but not God's enemies.

Prayer is just one component, albeit an indispensable one, in the personal transformation process. But authentic prayer is always informed and strengthened by immersing ourselves in Scripture.

Scripture

Prayer, apart from the Bible, will always slip into a vague spirituality whereby we treat God like a cosmic Santa Claus or Divine Therapist. Authentic prayer always drives us into Scripture, and naturally flows *from* our immersion in Scripture. Prayer involves not only speaking but listening as well, and it is in and through the Bible that God speaks to us most clearly.

It is important to understand that Jesus himself was a serious student of Scripture. As a young boy His parents found him in the temple "sitting among the teachers, listening to them and asking questions" (Lk 2:46). Jesus began his public ministry by spending forty days in the wilderness where Satan tempted him. Each of Jesus' refutations began with the words "it is written," which he followed up by quoting the Scriptures. Even Jesus' cry of dereliction from the cross—"My God, my God, why has thou forsaken me?"—was a direct quote from Psalm 22.

Jesus was rooted in the will of His Father because He was rooted in the Biblical narrative. The question is never "will our lives be rooted in a narrative," but rather "*what* narrative will our lives be rooted in?" We recall that we only have an identity in a *context*. The Bible is the context where God invites us to discover who we truly are.

The great challenge of our faith is not merely to intellectually grasp or define words like redemption, sin, salvation, grace, resurrection, and new creation. To the contrary, the challenge of our faith is for these to become the primary lens through which we view and interpret reality. Christian formation, therefore, is better understood as Christian *re*-formation. After all, the world has its own narratives, and they're all quite happy to give us a false identity by telling us who we are and what gives us value. As Bryan Smith explains:

> There are all kinds of narratives. Family narratives are the stories we learn from our immediate families. Our parents impart to us their worldview and their ethical system through stories. Key questions such as Who am I? Why am I here? Am I valuable? are answered early in the form of narrative. There are cultural narratives that we learn from growing up in a particular region of the world. From our culture we learn values (what is important, who is successful) in the form of stories and images. There are religious narratives—stories we hear from the pulpit, the classroom, and religious books that help us understand who God is, what God wants from us, and how we ought to live. Finally, there are Jesus' narratives, the stories and images Jesus tells us that reveal the character of God.[10]

We are all living out someone else's script. There is no getting around this reality. The question me must always be willing to ask is which script is most freeing and cosmically true? Which narrative best accounts for the deep questions

---

10 James Bryan Smith, *The Good and Beautiful God: Falling in Love with the God Jesus Knows* (Downer's Grove, IL: InterVarsity Press, 2009), 25.

of human existence and offers the most compelling vision for a joy-filled life of abundance? This is why Scripture is so important. It is God's script for our life and it tells us who we *really* are.

I am painfully aware of how tricky this all sounds. As Smith points out more often than not, the "religious narratives" we inherit are different than Jesus' narratives, even if we happened to grow up in a "Bible church." But two things are worth pointing out about Scripture's centrality. First, we believe that Scripture is breathed by the "Author of life" Himself (Acts 3:15). The words "author" and "authority" share the same root. We give the Bible priority because its vision for "the good life" comes from the One who has been bringing order out of chaos from the foundation of the world.

Second, Scripture is the only narrative that we can immerse ourselves in where, after a while, we hear God say, "You take the pen for a while." Although creation and redemption are both finished in God's mind, in a mystical way, as we enter the Story, we soon discover that we are characters and have been assigned a leading role! We come to know ourselves as co-laborers with God engaged in the meaningful work of anticipating God's New World, even though it has been finished in God's mind from the foundation of the world.

Self-Examination

Self-examination is the third critical component to a life of prayerful reflection. There is something about the knowledge that we are key actors in the drama of salvation that makes us want to clean up "our act." For example, when we gripe to God about people or circumstances, over time we realize that the primary problem is usually due to *us*. Or if nothing else, we play a role in the problem. Our lives will all get easier when we realize that our own behavior is all we have the capacity to change. This is why self-examination is so important.

Johann Wolfgang von Goethe once opined, "Know thyself? If I knew myself I'd run away!"[11] How different this is from Jesus who said, "Whoever loves the truth comes into the light" (Jn 3:21, paraphrase). There is so much about ourselves that we don't know that we *don't* know.[12] Jesus longs to show us these hidden parts of ourselves. There is no need for this to be scary. As St. Paul notes, "there is . . . no condemnation for those who are in Christ Jesus" (Rom 8:1). With condemnation and shame taken off the table, self-examination becomes an adventure in a life of continual learning.

Of course authentic self-examination always flows out of a commitment to prayer and Scripture. Self-knowledge is always the other side of God-knowledge. *Gnosis* (knowledge) of ourselves *dia* (through and through) is part of the reward of God's New World. The Risen Christ says, "To everyone who conquers . . . I will give a white stone, and on the white stone is written a new name that no one knows except the one who receives it" (Rev 2:17). The point is that when we stand before God, we will finally know ourselves fully, even as God has known us all along. This is what St. Paul is celebrating when he writes, "Then I will know fully, even as I have been fully known" (1 Cor 13:12). God knows and sees what our fully clothed glory self looks like. One day we will as well—and what a splendid sight that will be!

But in the meantime there is so much to explore, so much of our false self that needs to be purged away, and so many problems we are better off not experiencing because *we* are the ones that create them. Practically speaking, none of us wakes up and says, "Well, today I think I'll do the same stupid things I've been doing for decades!" and yet inevitably, by day's end, we do exactly that! Analytical psychologists have compared our conscious mind to a small boat floating on top of the ocean, or

---

11 http://thinkexist.com/quotation/-know_thyself-if_i_knew_myself_i-d_run/156585.html (accessed 10/4/13)

12 I borrow this phrase from "Faithwalking."

perhaps to the tip of a very large iceberg. There is so much that we don't know that we don't know about ourselves. It's not surprising that the etymology of the word *analyst* (the fancy word for a shrink) means to "dig up from underneath the surface." Prayer and Scripture not only give us the X of where we need to dig, but also the shovel, the water, and the necessary time to explore the deep places of our soul.

We all have areas of addition and brokenness in our lives that we are completely oblivious to. These areas of unconscious incompetence cause others and us great pain and unneeded frustration. We have so many wounds and unmet needs from childhood that keep us emotionally stuck in a painful pattern of not trusting God. This is why self-examination is so important. The devil we do know is *not* better than the new self we do not yet fully know. For example, this time last year I was completely unaware that my deep fear of abandonment can make me a pretty spineless people-pleaser. Until last year this important piece of knowledge fell in the realm of something I didn't know that I didn't know about myself. Now at least I can struggle to "speak the truth in love" (Eph 4:15) and lift this challenge up to God. Now I can pray about it. Now I can let Scripture speak to it. Before, I could do neither.

We will never make progress in the spiritual life if we do not look *within* even as we are looking without. There is no recipe for perpetual ignorance greater than being fully satisfied with our current opinions and knowledge about God, our world, and our selves.

Conclusion

It should be clear now that the young beach evangelist was right and wrong at the same time. On the one hand, salvation *is* the key to our existence and the opportunity of a lifetime. It is also "easy" in the sense that God executes, initiates, and sustains the whole thing. But at the same time, growing into the gift of salvation we have already received is to be our life's work. It may be simple, but it is anything but easy. Dietrich Bonhoeffer once remarked that when Christ calls a man, he bids him come and die. Being a follower of Jesus Christ demands everything. Of course, in giving Christ everything, we soon realize we actually never possessed anything in the first place. As Thomas Merton put it, "In order to become myself I must cease to be what I always thought I wanted to be, and in order to find myself I must go out of myself, and in order to live I have to die."[13] This is why the journey ahead is far from easy, and it most certainly will not fit on a business card.

Discussion Questions

1. In what sense is salvation "easy?" In what sense is salvation *not* easy?

2. How does one "grow" in the Christian life? What part, if any, do *we* play in the process?

3. What is the difference between "being productive" for God and abiding in Jesus and "bearing fruit"? What "fruit" should Christians bear?

4. When in your own life do you feel most "rooted" in God? When do you feel the least rooted in God?

5. Have you ever laid all your darkness and anger before God in prayer? What about such (naked) "honesty" with God makes you nervous?

6. Why is the Bible central to the Christian life? What does it mean to say Scripture has "authority"?

7. How well do you think you "know yourself"?

---

13 Merton, *New Seeds of Contemplation*, 47.

CHAPTER 7

Running the Race

Once upon a time, in a land of fear and confusion, some exciting news began to circulate. It was the good news of the big race. This race had long been anticipated by the people's ancient oracles, and the prophecies said that anyone who persevered in running this race would find restoration, support, and strength (1 Pet 5:10).

The day of the big race finally arrived. When the opening gun sounded, everyone began running with all of their might. But then something strange happened. One man, after just taking a few steps, fell to his knees and began to rejoice. "This is the happiest day of my life! I've crossed the starting line." The other runners all followed suit. They too stopped running and began to celebrate. "I'm a race runner! I'm a race runner!" This was their joyful shout. A huge celebration was taking place only a few feet from the starting line.

The joy of that opening gun eventually wore off. Slowly the racerunners got tired and bored. Some were confused and forgot where they were. Before long they were all back in the land of fear and confusion. And so as the story goes, they all stared at the sky and said, "What now?"[1]

---

1 This story I have adapted from *Adventures in Missing the Point: How the Culture-Controlled Church Neutered the Gospel* by Brian McLaren and Tony Campolo (Grand Rapids, MI: Zondervan, 2003).

What Now?

This story resonates with my own experience. I believe this also is an apt picture of where many Christians find themselves today. We remember the initial joy that came with first encountering Christ. The opening gun sounded and we took our first steps of faith with all the energy and zeal we could muster. But before we knew what hit us, we were back in the land of fear and confusion and stagnation wondering *what now?*

The Bible frequently compares the life of faith to a race. The author of Hebrews urges us to "run with perseverance the race that is set before us, looking to Jesus the pioneer and perfecter of our faith" (Heb 12:1–2). St. Paul, at the end of his life, boasts to young Timothy, "I have finished the race" (2 Tim 4:7). Jesus himself says we are to "strive to enter through the narrow door" (Lk 13:24). The Greek word translated "strive," which is used about a dozen times in the New Testament, alludes to the preparation one would have undergone in Jesus' day to train for the gymnastic games. The word strive was used to evoke images of an athlete who endeavors with strenuous zeal to obtain something infinitely precious. St. Paul articulates faith as a race in writing to the Corinthians.

> Do you not know that in a race the runners all compete, but only one receives the prize? Run in such a way that you may win it. Athletes exercise self-control in all things; they do it to receive a perishable wreath, but we an imperishable one. So I do not run aimlessly, nor do I box as though beating the air; but I punish my body and enslave it, so that after proclaiming to others I myself should not be disqualified. (1 Cor 9:24–27)

Following Jesus is not meant to be a part of our life. Increasingly, discipleship to Jesus must become our life. This doesn't mean that we can earn God's favor or that we can add even a spare button to the free garment of salvation that God in Christ has already bestowed upon us. But a large measure of intentionality is assumed on every page of the New Testament. Grace is most certainly opposed to earning. But it would be dead wrong to assert that grace leads to a *less* intentional life. Otherwise, Jesus Christ never would have told us to strive with all that we had. God's work is finished. Our work is not (Mt 24:13).

Vision

Vision in our own journey of spiritual and emotional maturation is essential. It is so very easy to profess faith in Christ and yet still live "tossed to and fro and blown about by every wind of doctrine" that the world imposes on us (Eph 4:14). But no one drifts into a life of greater freedom and love. As recipients of God's grace and believers in the Christian Gospel, we must consciously *intend* to grow into the garment of salvation that God has already bestowed onto us. And we can't just start running the race without considering our direction or else mapping our course at least to some degree. This thoughtful "mapping" work, which flows from our life of prayerful reflection, is what I mean by "vision."

Vision is an answer to the question, "What does God want to create in and through my life?" St. Paul says that each one of us is God's masterpiece (Eph 2:10). He also says that each Christian is a member of a greater body (Rom 12:5). No child of God is dispensable. Although our common vocation is to be transformed fully into the image of God's Son, this will look different for each one of us. Our respective journeys will have much in common. No one mirrors Jesus wearing the filthy rags of anger, jealousy, lust, or self-indulgence. But God is shaping each of his children as a mini-masterpiece. When God's new

Day dawns we will all come together as one to form the ultimate Masterpiece—Jesus' Bride, the Church.

While I believe that whatever vision we have for our growth into Christlikeness will necessarily encompass our actions, I find it far more helpful to make progress in the race when we think of vision work in terms of our character.

Why We Struggle

The reason so many of us struggle to get past the starting line in our faith is that our minds have been poisoned by our western, consumerist view of "the good life." After all, Jesus and the American dream offer us the same thing—"abundant life" (Jn 10:10). In both cases the end game is the same. The goal is for us to thrive and to come fully alive. The goal is human flourishing. However, when we compare Jesus' view and the Western view of the good life, the *means* to that end could not be more different. Our problem is that we tend to conflate these two views, which is the very thing Jesus warned us about (Mt 6:24). No wonder we get tripped up! It's impossible to run in two different directions at the same time.[2]

Our Western, consumer-oriented culture says that abundance of life is found in acquiring as much stuff as possible, achieving as much as possible, and eliminating all pain. Virtue is about being nice and good. God is responsible for rewarding us with health, wealth, and longevity of life if we are nice and good. The point of life is not to grow in grace, which involves growing pains (Heb 12:6; Jn 15:2), but to grow in a life of ease and convenience. In our culture's view of the "the good life," suffering and sacrifice are to be avoided at all costs—a big problem for a faith that has the crucifix as its chief symbol.

---

2 I am indebted to my friend Jim Herrington and the Faithwalking community for getting clear in my mind the need to distinguish between these two competing views for "the good life."

The vast majority of Western Christians, including myself, keep trying to have our cake and eat it too. We have bought into the Gospel of consumerism hook, line, and sinker. We say, "I haven't done anything wrong," and then ask, "Why would God let this happen to me?" We do not see ourselves as wrecked people in the midst of a ruined world, who desperately need redemption, but rather as contract workers who have honored our end of the bargain and think that God must owe us a pain-free and problem-free life in return.

The marketplace has also infiltrated our churches. I recently drove past one church that advertised "thirty-minute worship." I realized that thirty-minute worship is a response not to a need but to a *want*. The pastor knows his people are "shopping" for a church and he needs to make sure his product is competitive. He knows his people are tired, work too much, and that they are not getting enough sleep. After all, pursuing the American dream is exhausting. His people want an extra thirty minutes. They want twice the worship experience in half the time. What they want is a better *product*. So, to remain competitive, the pastor "sold" thirty-minute worship to his congregation.

I don't mean to pick on anyone. I know how deeply consumerism drives my behavior. I so badly want to want what I currently *do not want*—namely, to sacrifice my own life of ease and convenience to bless the people in my life, community, and world that simply do not have hope. Currently, I want a fat 401(k) more than I want to bless the homeless. I want to want what I know I currently do not want. I'm a consumer of religious goods and services just like everyone else.

I don't condemn myself or anyone else, because I know Jesus doesn't condemn us. But I am interested in learning to want what I currently do not want, and that learning requires a commitment to the truth. My hope is that we will learn to tell the truth about the ways that we have unwittingly bought into our culture's view of abundant life, and have been left paralyzed and frustrated at the starting line of the Christian faith. Only in being honest can we give Jesus' vision of abundant life the hearing it deserves.

Jesus' View

Jesus' view of the fully human, fully alive life is rooted in both our creation and redemption. The apex of abundant life as Jesus sees it consists of authentic and intimate relationships with God and each other, as well as in doing meaningful work that glorifies God, builds on our gifts, and demands our very best effort.

Our situation is not the same as Adam's situation. We live east of Eden. The abundant life is found in losing our "life" so that we can receive it anew *in* Jesus Christ. We lose our ego and gain our soul.

This is where *vision work* comes into play. I believe Jesus has a clear vision for our future, fully clothed glory self. The new self simply *is* the garment of salvation. Our new self is first and foremost *God's* vision, and yet, paradoxically, we cannot shirk doing our own vision work in conversation with God. Apart from such work we cannot die to the "self" we inherit from our culture, which has largely been shaped by our family, tribe, and the values of our world. And as St. Paul says, "We must grow up in every way into him who is the head, into Christ, from whom the whole body, joined and knit together by every ligament with which it is equipped, as each part is working properly, promotes the body's growth in building itself up in love" (Eph 4:15–16). This happens to the extent that we are willing to lose our small, worldly life to find a garment that is new and infinitely better fitting in Jesus. In Jesus' own words, "If any want to become my followers, let them deny themselves and take up their cross and follow me. For those who want to save their life will lose it, and those who lose their life for my sake will find it" (Mt 16:24–25).

Unlike our cultural view that says "if you want abundant life you have to grab for abundant life," Jesus says, "if you want abundant life you have to lose the *small life* you cling to so tightly." We must die and be resurrected. Our death, which sacramentally is enacted in baptism, is our gateway to new and abundant life. We strive for God's righteousness, which kills our self-righteous ego, and we find abundant life in the process.

A Personal Vision for our Growth into Christlikeness

The reason it is so necessary to point out the difference between Jesus' view of where abundant life is found and the cultural view is that, unless we consciously distinguish between these two views, our vision for growth will be blurred. We will unwittingly be trying to serve two masters (Mt 6:24).

Doing vision work is not always easy or fun. This work is complicated by the fact that ultimately we are all pursuing the same thing—the fully clothed glory self, which will only be given to us fully as a *gift* in God's new world. But, as we have already said, we can and must anticipate our "new clothes" now and even proactively co-labor with the One who dresses us for the feast (1 Cor 3:9). This requires that, as we engage in the continual practice of self-examination and prayer, we ponder deeply what renewal will look like in *our* own life. We use our imaginative faculties to answer some basic questions, such as: If I let God have His way with me, what specifically will my life look like in one year? In five years? In twenty-five? How will my character be changed? How will I function differently in my marriage? With my children? With my co-workers? What habits might God ask me to drop and pick up? What gifts do I have that can be used to offer hope to the least and the lost? What abilities might I need to develop? Where do I still need healing? What is it about myself that I still don't know that creates consistent messes in my life and in the lives of people I love? Where do I still not trust God? What is my dream? What is God's dream for me? Answering these, and many similar questions, is precisely what casting a personal vision for our growth in Christlikeness will entail. However, because we're all very different, growth in our lives will always look different. Two people can and often are quite similar. But no two people are ever the same.

For example, Bob and Carl habitually disobey God's command to "speak the truth in love" (Eph 4:15). Bob is confrontational and self-righteous. When he perceives that someone has wronged him or someone he loves, Bob is quick to let them know about it. Bob boasts that he is ruthlessly honest as if his behavior were a virtue. The only problem is that Bob enjoys telling people off. He subconsciously looks for and even creates opportunities to "set people straight." Bob is not competent at speaking the truth in love.

Carl, on the other hand, is nice, sensitive, and well liked. He hates offending people and Carl wants nothing more than to keep the peace. As a result, Carl is quick to let people invade his boundaries. If Carl's friend tells a racist joke, he will laugh even though he really doesn't think it's funny. Carl boasts that his gift is "meeting people where they are." But deep down Carl knows that he hasn't yet learned the skill of speaking the truth in love.

Bob and Carl have the same vocation—to "grow up in every way into him who is the head, into Christ" (Eph 4:15). Their ultimate vision is also the exact same, which is the fully clothed glory self. But, Bob and Carl's differences mean that their personal vision for their growth in Christlikeness will look much different from one another. Such is why the new clothes we have in Christ are never a "one-size fits all" garment. They are tailor made for each of us. Fortunately, God is an extremely competent Tailor.

The Twofold Nature of Vision

Vision work is about seeing our life before God more clearly. If we get glasses and see objects more clearly, we say that our vision has improved. When leaders of churches and organizations speak about vision, it is usually in reference to something they would like to achieve in the future, such as "in the next two years we will have a fully developed feeding program where we can minister to the homeless population of our city." But when I speak of our personal vision of transformation into Christlikeness, I am referring to two very specific things.

First, I do indeed mean *foresight* when I refer to vision. We must look into the future and perceive what is not. We must imagine what we will look like as we become more obedient to Jesus. Carl will look less like a people-pleaser. Bob will look more like a people-pleaser. God has a preferred future for the men and women we are to be. We must get really clear on God's preferred future for our lives. This is central to our vision work.

But there is also a second and typically overlooked aspect of vision. The second aspect of vision is to perceive what currently is. We must tell the truth, without shame or fear or condemnation, about the sort of person we *presently* are. It is easy to get excited about where we want to go. Telling the truth about where we are right now is much more difficult, and perhaps even important. I think this is what the church originally meant by the phrase "confession" before that became such a loaded word.

Striving to Close the Gap

Jesus knows vision work is difficult. Otherwise, Jesus never would have told us to strive. If the work were easy, Jesus would have told us to "coast into the Kingdom" or perhaps to "ride the current of the Spirit." But Jesus didn't say these things. He told us to strive because Jesus knew that growing up spiritually would be difficult. In fact, Jesus called it a *daily* crucifixion (Lk 9:23).

And there is a reason telling the truth, which vision work entails, is so painful. The moment we start plotting where we are now in the spiritual life, as well as where we hope to be, we become painfully aware that a gap exists between God's preferred vision for our lives and the current reality. This gap tends to deflate us. We see the gap as a challenge and source of pain. But here is what I believe. "To grow up in every way into Him who is the head," we must see the gap as the very source of our energy to keep striving for God's Kingdom. The gap between the acknowledged present and God's preferred future creates "spiritual tension." The gap is where the Spirit of God meets us to bring order from the chaos of our lives. God lives in your gap.

It is human nature to want to close gaps once we see them. Our species doesn't do well with tension and we long to do away with it. But when it pertains to the spiritual life, there is something we need to see. There are only two ways to eliminate the tension associated with a gap. We can lower the vision and move it closer to our current reality. "I don't need to lose twenty pounds. Five is a much more realistic goal." Or we can work to move the current reality towards the vision, which in the spiritual life, we call faithfulness. Carl can either say, "The truth really isn't that big of a deal. The world needs more nice guys." Or he can learn to speak the truth in love. But once Carl identifies that gap in his life and authentically shares the truth of the gap with a community of people committed to the spiritual renovation of their insides, one thing Carl cannot do is ignore it. One way or another, Carl will choose to resolve the spiritual tension that his personal vision work has created. He will lower the vision so that it is aligned with current reality (quitting).

Or he will take steps to move current reality towards his vision (striving).

That is why personal vision work is so powerful. Once you see something you cannot un-see it.

A Principle-Centered Life

We can now safely speak of what personal vision work looks like in practice. As we engage in prayerful reflection, self-examination, and truth telling from a life increasingly immersed in Scripture and community, personal vision work will lead to *Christ-centered* principles by which we are to live. Such principles are practical ways we anticipate God's new world, a compass that re-orients us when our loincloths create a mess in our lives.

It is important to see that we all have something or someone at the center of our lives. Our center guides our actions and serves as the basis of our security. Our center is our "functional god." Now obviously for the Christian, Jesus Christ is the center of our life. But to leave the matter here will leave us in a foggy maze unable to see what *we*, as individual disciples, are to strive for. Therefore, as our prayerful self-examination brings us in touch with our habitual areas of stumbling and addiction, we can thoughtfully and prayerfully articulate the principles we believe will enable us to grow up spiritually as we strive to live into them.

Much of our problem stems from the fact that we say that Jesus is our center but functionally speaking Jesus is *not* the center of our life. Common pseudo centers (or what the Bible calls "idols") include our job, our possessions, the Church, our spouse, our children, our friends, our enemies, or perhaps pleasure. This is not an exhaustive list. And these many pseudo centers are really nothing more than different variations of how we ensure that our loincloth-disguised ego remains front and center.

But if we are to lose our life for the sake of the Gospel so that we might find it anew in Jesus, Christ-centered principles that describe the *sort* of people we want to be will greatly aid us in our journey. For example, one of St. Paul's guiding principles could be stated as follows: "I will always discern and do what is pleasing to the Lord Jesus Christ" (2 Cor 5:9; Col 1:10; Eph 5:10). If you read his letters carefully, it becomes clear that Paul had dozens of principles that guided his life as a missionary. They oozed out of his writing like sweat from his pores.

It is important to understand that Christ-centered principles are not mere goals, nor are they rooted in our ideals. Rather, Biblical principles are solidly rooted in how "things really are." When we break them, they break us. That's how truth works. Earlier we used the example of the "truth" of gravity. We may or may not believe in gravity. But if we jump off of our balcony, gravity's truth will impose itself upon us.

So it is with Biblical principles. You may not believe that being slow to anger is where abundant life is found (Eph 4:26; Mt 5:22; Prov 15:18). But if Bob doesn't come to terms with the anger that fuels his confrontational personality, he will forfeit the intimate relationships God created him for and his anger will poison his work. So it is with Carl. His failure to be truthful has created a web of pseudo relationships. At the center of Carl's life is not concern for the other, but a desire to protect his fragile ego. Bob's and Carl's mutual incompetence at speaking the truth in love is breaking them apart in a million different ways. This is true whether they choose to acknowledge it or not.

Christ-centered principles are not ways we make ourselves worthy before God. These are not laws that, if followed, will make us "righteous." They are grace-fueled descriptions of what we will increasingly come to look like to the extent that we truly believe that God has already made us worthy. Put differently, Christ-centered principles are means to the end of telling the truth—the truth of who we already are in Christ (*Iustus*) and the truth of who we presently experience ourselves to be (*Peccator*).

If the word "principle" is a stumbling block to you and reeks of anti-grace moralizing, well, I get it. And so think of what follows not so much as principles but as grace-centered descriptions of who we would be if we knew deep in our bones the truth that in Jesus Christ we are already worthy, justified, that we have nothing at all to prove and that there is nothing we can do, including recoiling at the word "principle," that can ever separate us from the love of Christ. Vision work is about envisioning who we already are. It reminds us of what's true and gives us a direction in which to run, and then reminds us that it's not our own running that saves us. These principles are not so much virtues as they are practical graces. And yet, the mystery of our faith is that we are still told to strive for what only can be received as a gift. They are *both* ways we "root" and things we "fruit."

This is how it looks in practice from a few of the Christ-centered principles that guide my life. This list of ten principles is not exhaustive. Below each principle is the truth about where I currently am spiritually. Between the principle and my current reality is a gap, which creates spiritual tension in my life. Now that I see this tension I cannot *un-see* it and this forces me to choose. Will I lower the vision? "I am already saved. This isn't important." Or, by renewing my mind daily with the Christ-centered principles that enable me to anticipate my fully clothed glory self (Rom 12:2), will I partner with God and move the current reality towards the vision? That is the choice I face every single day.

My Guiding Principles

1. I am radically self-compassionate (Rom 8:1; 1 Cor 4:3). *If I make a mistake or fall short of*

perfection, I crucify myself. I don't always feel
that I am saved by sheer grace. In the deep
recesses of my heart I try to earn my salvation
and I sometimes hate myself because I can't.

2. I welcome pain as a gift that brings consciousness
    and growth (Rom 5:3–5; Heb 12:6). *I experience
    pain as a problem and not as an opportunity to
    grow into a life of deeper joy and obedience.
    When my needs go unmet, I usually blame the
    people I unrealistically expect to meet those
    needs. The usual result is a seething anger. At God
    and at other people.*

3. I value relationships over achievements (Mt 22:39;
    Jn 15:13). *My ego is nourished by accolades. I am
    not sure I care how much I achieve as long as it
    is more than you. I make a name for myself by
    building a tower of accomplishments (Gen 11:4). I
    am a Martha and not a Mary (Lk 10:42). I often feel
    that people who are comfortable sitting at Jesus'
    feet are lazy.*

4. I do not fix or condemn people (Mt 7:3; Rom
    14:4). *I think people's greatest problem is that
    they don't ask me for help. Listening to people's
    problems is a means to an end. My job is to
    straighten them out. Of course no one else sees
    that and so I condemn them.*

5. I clearly define my beliefs to others (Eph 4:15; 1
    Pet 3:15). *I am Carl. I value peace over progress
    and pseudo relationships without pain to intimate
    relationships that involve pain. I can be anyone
    you need me to be and am skilled at using
    Scripture to justify my behavior (1 Cor 9:20).*

6. I am not in a hurry (Lk 8:15; 2 Pet 3:8). *I am impatient and get angry when something takes a long time. When people ask me how things are going, I brag by telling them how busy life is as if exhaustion were a status symbol. When I "waste" a day by not being productive, I get depressed. I can easily feel contempt for people who interrupt me.*

7. I relinquish my whole self to the will of God (Lk 22:42; Rom 14:8). *I frantically try to control every aspect of my life. Deep down I do not believe God is competent or that He can be trusted to meet my deepest needs. I am the captain of my own ship. I pray "thy will be done" and then move on with my plan.*

8. I am courageously vulnerable (Jas 5:16; 2 Cor 11:30). *I put my best face forward. I hide my true self. I wear different masks for different occasions. I don't talk about how fearful, lonely, and scary life can be. I'm scared of what people would say if they knew I thought such things.*

9. I am more grateful than I am angry (Col 3:16; 1 Thess 5:18). *I am more angry than thankful. I often feel I "deserve" more than life has given me. Life can feel more like a misery than a mystery at times. I am hypersensitive to someone's snub, while a kind word or an act of service recedes from my conscious mind after only a few minutes.*

10. I do not gossip or lie (2 Tim 2:16; Mt 12:36). *What is there really to talk about but other people's sins, scandals, and stories, especially when my "true self" is off limits? There is at present a direct correlation on any given day between the number of words I speak and sins I commit.*

A Commitment to Lifelong Learning

I did not come up with these Christ-centered guiding principles overnight, nor did I learn to "tell the truth about myself" overnight. This work emerged out of my own commitment to a life of prayerful reflection grounded in the Gospel. It has been tested in community as I seek to obey the vision I believe Jesus has given me for my own personal spiritual growth.

What I have discovered is that a commitment to the process is more important than the product. It is not so much what our vision is, but what the vision *does*. Vision work makes you see the gap and creates the spiritual tension that is necessary for growth in Christlikeness to take place.

This is why discipleship is ultimately a commitment to lifelong learning. A more accurate understanding of the Greek word typically translated disciple (*mathetes*) is the word apprentice. An apprentice is someone who intentionally spends an enormous amount of time in the presence of a master to learn his skill or trade. So it is in the life of Christian discipleship. The Master is Jesus. The skill Jesus imparts is the art of living in God's new world with Jesus' own heart and character. The fruit of the process is growth in Christlikeness. As Jesus himself once put it, "It is enough for the disciple to be like the teacher" (Mt 10:25).

This is why growth and a commitment to learning are at the heart of our Christian faith. To be a disciple is to approach our life as a creative work. It is simultaneously true that we are God's Masterpiece (Eph 2:10) and also that the Chief Artist has given us the brush and said, "Paint!" We co-labor with God. We are always responsible for who we become, which is why we must learn the art of seeing. Not only is it important to always be sharpening our values and principles, but we must also learn the freedom of confessing what is true for us now. This is why disciples never "arrive" on this side of God's new world. For the apprentice, the growth that takes place on the journey is always part of the reward.

Intention

All the vision work in the world, of course, is meaningless without a firm intention to die daily and finish the race. Personal transformation into Christlikeness is a complete life overhaul. Merely rejecting our culture's view of abundant life is itself something few of us really intend to do—myself included. But in my experience, the more you let Jesus *in,* the less power you have to keep Jesus out. Jesus isn't always a polite Guest. He tends to invite himself "in" without being asked (Lk 19:5). He tinkers with things in our life we would prefer He leave alone. He shines light into our darkness, creates gaps, and those gaps create spiritual tension. And Jesus will continue to generate this tension in our life until we become the fully clothed glory self that He had in mind long before we heard His call. This is how C. S. Lewis puts it:

> Christ says "Give me All. I don't want so much of your time and so much of your money and so much of your work: I want You. I have not come to torment your natural self, but to kill it. No half-measures are any good. I don't want to cut off a branch here and a branch there, I want to have the whole tree down. I don't want to drill the tooth, or crown it, or stop it, but to have it out. Hand over the natural self, all the desires which you think innocent as well as the ones you think wicked—the whole outfit. I will give you a new self instead. In fact, I will give you Myself: my own will shall become yours."[3]

---

3 Lewis, *Mere Christianity,* 196–197.

And here we have the essence of the Christian Gospel—Jesus' intention is to kill us. The mask wearing "us" that stresses and struts about in the loincloths we have learned to wear to survive in the world needs to be killed. And there is only one thing I know for certain that such a process entails: pain. We must ask if we truly intend to go through with it.

Pain

Jesus once compared himself to a physician that came to treat really sick people. We usually hear that and jump straight to the good news that we're "all better" in Christ and forget the poignancy of the metaphor, namely, that to get better we often initially feel much worse. In Jesus' day, "anesthesiology" wasn't a career path. People in Jesus' day knew that going to the doctor might make them feel worse before it made them feel better.

At one point Jesus asked a man who had been sick for thirty-eight years, "Do you *want* to be made well?" If you read the text carefully, the sick man doesn't say yes but rather offers Jesus an excuse for *why* he is still sick (see Jn 5:2–5). Getting well is not always a fun process, especially for a false self whose chief guiding principle is, "Grow in a life of ease and convenience." For example, consider the nature of going to rehab. One doesn't go to rehab to get well, but to have a breakdown. And that is exactly what Jesus longs to accomplish in our life. Jesus wants to break down the old self we're addicted to, and replace it with a new one. As Jesus himself says:

> If any want to become my followers, let them deny themselves and take up their cross daily and follow me. For those who want to save their life will lose it, and those who lose their life for my sake will save it. What does it profit them if they gain the whole world, but lose or forfeit themselves? (Lk 9:23–25)

Taking up our Cross

It is hard to speak about the mystery of what it actually means to take up our cross. In my experience the cross is something that takes *us up*, as we grow deeper in our life of discipleship. The cross is something we come to welcome only as we see its redemptive purpose in our own life. But one thing we can say for certain is that the cross is not an option for the person who intends to grow in Christlikeness. We must all come to say with St. Paul, "I have been crucified with Christ" (Gal 2:19).

The late Ed Friedman once noted, "There is no way out of a chronic condition without being willing to go through a temporarily more acute phase."[4] He meant that fundamental change often feels worse before it feels better. Recall the image of Psalm 1 where growth in Christlikeness is about spreading the roots of our soul deep into Living Water (Jn 4:14). We must remember that roots are where nerves are found, and that often times, pouring water on a cut stings even as it cleanses the wound.

I make such a fuss about firmly intending to grow because we've been formed in a world that values comfort over maturity and compartmentalizes faith as yet another means to the end of a more comfortable life. We have inherited a quick-fix attitude. We value symptom relief more than we do going to the roots of whatever underlying causes bring about our symptoms. But the condition of our lives at present, spiraling away from God in a cycle of sin, shame, and addiction, is in fact a chronic condition. We are unconscious of just how incompetent we are at living the sort of abundant life Jesus came to give us. If we are to enjoy the newness of life Jesus offers us, He will lead us to the cross.

Pain, Not Harm

Jesus will never harm us. Pain and harm are not synonymous. Jesus expects that following Him will bring pain with it. Jesus

---

4 Friedman, *A Failure of Nerve*, 84.

told us we would be pruned (Jn 15:2). Here we have the image of a knife cutting off excess debris from our heart. God's intention is to throw us in the fire until we are refined inside and out, fully and completely like Jesus (Mal 3:3). And meanwhile we are assured that these growing pains are not a sign of God's anger but His love, "for the Lord disciplines those whom he loves, and chastises every child whom he accepts" (Heb 12:6).

This is why there is a huge difference between pain and harm. Jesus would never do anything to us, or allow anything to happen to us, that would cause us ultimate harm. Nothing could ever separate us from His love or stop His work from being completed in our lives. As St. Paul put it, "Neither death, nor life, nor angels, nor rulers, nor things present, nor things to come, nor powers, nor height, nor depth, nor anything else in all creation, will be able to separate us from the love of God in Christ Jesus our Lord" (Rom 8:38–39).

Is Discipleship Hard or Easy?

This of course makes us ask, "If I truly intend to follow Jesus, knowing the cost, is it worth it?" This is a fair question that each of us must wrestle with.

Jesus once said that, "Everyone who commits sin is a slave to sin" (Jn 8:34). This teaching meshes with what we know about sin from chapter 2. Sin is a hard life. Always dumping the bucket of our soul into empty wells is exhausting and painful. It is exhausting to manage the fear, cynicism, irritability, frustration, and isolation that accompany an egocentric life that competes with everyone else for our share of the pie. Jesus, on the other hand, offers us life in abundance, which we receive through grace and increasingly experience as we risk practicing greater and greater obedience. If abundant life is *not* found in Jesus, then I am not sure losing our life with Him and for Him is worth it.

But, if Jesus was right, regardless of what discipleship *does* cost us, non-discipleship will always cost more. As Dallas Willard puts it:

> Non-discipleship costs abiding peace, a life penetrated throughout by love, faith that sees everything in the light of God's overriding governance for good, hopefulness that stands firm in the most discouraging of circumstances, power to do what is right and withstand the forces of evil. In short, it costs exactly that abundance of life Jesus said he came to bring (Jn 10:10). The cross-shaped yoke of Christ is after all an instrument of liberation and power to those who live in it with him and learn the meekness and lowliness of heart that brings rest to the soul.[5]

Put differently, our transformation into Christlikeness is the key to unlocking the life we have always wanted. And so the question is never can we afford to follow Jesus. The question is always: can we afford not to?

Means

This now bring us full circle. As we engage in a life of prayerful reflection and develop the habit of cultivating a vision for what our growth in Christlikeness looks like, we must commit to a life of radical obedience in the context of an authentic faith community where courageous vulnerability is the norm.

Community and Obedience

An indispensable aspect of our personal transformation into Christlikeness is remaining connected to an authentic community where vulnerability and transparency are the norm. We

---

5 Dallas Willard, *The Great Omission: Reclaiming Jesus's Essential Teachings on Discipleship* (Oxford, UK: Monarch Books, 2006), 9.

recall that part of our answer to *the big why* is that we were created for intimacy with God and other people. Originally there was no pretense, hiding, or masks. Adam and Eve were naked and unashamed. If we are to grow up spiritually, this is something the disciple of Jesus must come to love and value. Metaphorically speaking we must get naked with one another and show our true selves, warts and all. An adventurous spirit of learning must replace condemnation. We must tell the truth to other people about aspects of our life where, at present, we are struggling to obey Jesus' leading and learn to confess such things without an ounce of shame or fear.

This is something most of us find so difficult. Shame is something we all wrestle with, and the essence of shame is to want nothing more than to hide and cover up the darkness we find inside of us. We have learned to cover our true selves with loincloths and perfect an image to display to the world. The problem with the image we have so carefully crafted is simply that *our image* is not real. It is a false self, created from our instinctual drive to hide, feel safe, and avoid pain. As a result we all have *three* selves that we can identify: our public self, our private self, and our secret self.[6]

Our public self is the image we put on display to the world. It differs depending on the setting we find ourselves in. We might act one way at church and another way at an office happy hour. The public self is largely the person we have learned to be to ensure others do not reject us and to secure for ourselves what we think we need from others to remain happy and comfortable. Not all of the public self is "false," though most of it is since it has in large part been formed, not from a set of prayerfully developed principles, but rather from patterns we developed to deal with the unmet needs and wounds of childhood.

---

6 This distinction between three selves (public, private, and secret) is also an insight I borrow from the Faithwalking community.

Our private self is an aspect of us that only those closest to us are privy to. For example, Emily and I sometimes get goofy and start doing impressions of our favorite celebrities. We're both pretty bad. These are aspects of our private self. We show certain people portions of ourselves that aren't "appropriate" in public.

But then there is our secret self, which consists of those places within us that only we know about. This is where shame lives. The secret self is also where some of our deepest hopes, fears, and aspirations live. This is the self that God knows inside and out, though there is much to our secret self that we ourselves do *not* know. This is why self-examination is really better understood as "secret self" examination.

This is where authenticity, vulnerability, and transparency come into play. We were created for intimate relationships with God and each other, and this will necessarily mean coming out of hiding and learning to integrate our public, private, and secret selves into one coherent "self" guided by a set of prayerfully constructed Christ-centered principles and held together by grace. In God's new world we will only have *one* self and it will be on full display to God and everyone else. And it will be glorious—a fully clothed glory self. This is the direction we must move as disciples of Jesus: toward one, renewed Christlike self before God and others.

Authenticity with God

This will no doubt mean greater transparency and authenticity with God. We cannot have intimacy with God without being honest. If we feel deceived and lied to by God, we need to let Him know (Jer 20:7). If we really don't believe God can heal us, we need to tell God (Mk 9:24). If all we care about is losing our job, we dare not dress up for God and pray for world peace. Prayer without authentic transparency is yet another form of hiding. And hiding, as well as the shame that fuels it, is the gremlin that keeps us stuck in the first place.

Authenticity with Others

Authenticity with God is relatively easy. We don't have to physically look at God or see His reaction to what we lay before Him. Showing our secret self to others is much more difficult and requires that we be courageously vulnerable with one another.

Courage and vulnerably are not words we tend to associate with one another. We associate courage with bravery, and vulnerability we tie to weakness. But in the Christian Gospel, and especially in light of Jesus' sacrificial death on the cross, courage and vulnerability are forever wed. Courage and vulnerability go hand in hand. According to Brené Brown:

> The root of the word courage is *cor*—the Latin word for heart. In one of its earliest forms, the word courage had a very different definition than it does today. Courage originally meant "To speaks one's mind by telling all one's heart."[7]

This is perfectly in step with the message of the Christian Gospel. When Jesus Christ rose victoriously from the dead, His resurrected glory self still had scars and wounds from His crucifixion (Jn 20:27). His wounds were not removed but transformed into a source of healing for His disciples. In the same way, our strength is found not in hiding our weaknesses, but in being courageously vulnerable and putting our wounds, warts, and worries on full display to others on the same journey as us.

St. Paul fully grasped this principle. The church he planted at Corinth was being led astray by "super apostles" that boasted

---

7 Brown, *The Gifts of Imperfection*, 12.

of their god-like strengths and competencies they thought deemed them worthy of Christian leadership. Paul wrote 2 Corinthians, at least in part, to respond to their boasting. "If I must boast," he said, "I will boast of the things that show my weakness" (2 Cor 11:30). Paul knew that in telling the truth about himself, he would simultaneously be proclaiming the truth about God. Namely, that "Christ died for the ungodly" (Rom 5:6).

Experiencing Grace

If we are to grow into Christlikeness and run with perseverance the race that is set before us, we must return to the dress code in Eden and get naked with one another. It is important to practice this in the context of a small Christian community. This community must value extending grace and truth. It is not wise to show our secret self at all times and in all places. Such is the nature of our fallen world. Plus, vulnerability and over sharing are not the same things. However, in God's new world our whole self will be on display for all to see. *More* disclosure is the direction that being a disciple of Jesus will take us. This is true for two very important reasons.

First, there is a big difference between understanding God's grace and experiencing God's grace. Only the experience of God's grace will transform us into mature disciples. We can read about grace and preach about grace until we are blue in the face. But unless we experience grace, we will not be transformed. There is something powerful about confessing to other believers our shame, fear, and failures, as well as our deepest hopes and aspirations. Grace cannot be described but only experienced. To show a fellow pilgrim your secret self, and to have them show you theirs, is to be reminded of our common journeying and of the great truth that not one of us is alone in our sins.

Second, our self-knowledge will remain limited until we get in the habit of disclosing ourselves fully to others. As we become less afraid of revealing our secret self, we will at the same time become more eager to learn about our secret self. We all have the experience of seeing the horrible flaws in others, especially those we love, that they haven't yet owned up to in themselves. The good news for disciples is that our friends see clearly our flaws as well, especially the flaws we are in complete denial about. When we are in authentic community with others, we do not just invite them to extend grace, but also the truth of what they see in us. We flat out assume that there are things we need to repent of and that by not repenting we are missing out on the abundant life we seek in following Jesus. We cannot repent unless we know what keeps us stuck, and we cannot know such things until we have invited our fellow pilgrims to tell us the truth about what we at present do not see in ourselves.

We will not grow into the full stature of Christ apart from authentic community where transparency and vulnerability are the norm. I don't mean *just* going to church. I mean having a group of people where we are in the habit of taking off our masks to confess where we need to be pruned by the Father. For example, I'm a control freak because at a deep, deep level, part of me doesn't believe that God is competent. And on top of that, my fear of abandonment can make me a pretty spineless people-pleaser. I also have an anger problem. These are things I did not know about myself last year. God only knows what I'll discover next, but I know I won't discover it, or grow out of it, alone. As Henri Nouwen has said, "Only when we dare to lay down our protective shields and trust each other enough to confess our shared weakness and need can we live a fruitful life together."[8]

---

8 Nouwen, *Lifesigns*, 53.

Only in becoming small and weak and vulnerable could God save us. Surely this must mean something for what it means to be a follower of Jesus.

Discussion Questions

1. In what sense is faith like a "race" we must run? In what sense is faith *not* like a race at all?

2. How does Jesus' view of "abundant life" differ from the view offered by the Western world?

3. Name one (negative) aspect of your character (i.e., a place where your spiritual/emotional immaturity is prone to surface) that you believe Jesus wants to "work on" with you. How does this aspect of your character impair your relationships?

4. Jesus said that to follow him we had to die daily. What does "dying daily" mean to you? What role does pain have in the spiritual life?

5. How does one come to "intend" to follow Jesus? How can we strengthen our intention to follow Jesus?

6. How would you define "vulnerability" and "transparency?" Are they an important part of the Christian life? If so, *why?*

7. What is the difference between understanding God's grace and experiencing God's grace? How does one experience grace?

CHAPTER 8

Growing Taller While Becoming Smaller

The hardest decision I have ever made was whether or not to commit a friend of mine to a mental institution. I was in Europe for the spring semester of my junior year of college. It was there I met a friend named Dan. Over a period of several weeks, Dan began acting unusually isolated and withdrawn. He became increasingly erratic, and his odd behavior escalated until one day he had a violent, panicky meltdown. To make a long story short, my friend Tucker and I had Dan arrested and institutionalized, and Dan remained in a European mental facility until his parents could arrange for his release.

Of course you're no doubt wondering why we would do such a thing. The nature of Dan's problem was that he actually believed that he was Jesus Christ, the central figure around whom the world revolved. Dan was diagnosed with what some psychologists refer to as a full-blown Messiah complex.[1]

To the best of my knowledge, there isn't much consensus on what causes a full-blown Messiah complex. However,

---

1 John Ortberg tells a similar story in *The Life You Have Always Wanted: Spiritual Disciplines for Ordinary People* (Grand Rapids, MI: Zondervon, 1997), 107.

psychologists agree its primary symptom is a false sense of security and self-confidence. Many people believe that a full-blown
Messiah complex. is nothing more than a hyper-exaggerated
form of human arrogance. This terrifies me because our default
setting is to live as if *we* were the central figure around whom
the world revolved. We build *our* life around *our* loincloths so
that *our* ego will feel significant. As John Calvin once remarked,
"each individual, by flattering himself, bears a kind of kingdom
in his breast."[2] Put differently, we're all prone to make life
about *us*. We all have a Messiah complex. It's just a matter of
degree.

Christians have long known that we suffer from a Messiah
complex and we've given our disease a name: pride. The sin of
pride is literally the "oldest one in the book." In chapter 2 we
looked at the *fruit* of the fall (shame, isolation, and the false
self), but not the *root* of the fall. The snake tempted Eve as she
pondered whether or not to take the forbidden fruit. "You will
not die; for God knows that when you eat of it your eyes will
be opened, and you will be like God" (Gen 3:4–5). Adam and
Eve wanted to be *like* God. The only problem is that they failed
to understand what the God of the universe was actually like.
They thought they had to grasp and fight and claw to take their
place at the center of the universe.

So here we see the nature of Adam and Eve's problem. They
wanted, and we want, to be like God without ever stopping to
ponder what God is actually like. We want to be the center of
the universe. Pride is the erroneous belief that we need to make
ourselves the center of the universe to be happy. Pride is spiritual cancer. It eats up the very possibility of love, happiness, or
even common sense. Pride isn't a mere dilemma; it is a deadly,
delusional disease.

---

2 John Calvin, *Golden Booklet of the True Christian Life*, translated by Henry J. Van Andel
(Grand Rapids: Baker Book House, 1977), 28.

But pride is only half the problem. There's a very specific ingredient that pride feeds on to stay alive. Pride needs food, and its daily bread is fear. In the same way that a fire cannot exist in the absence of oxygen, pride cannot exist apart from a healthy dose of fear. Adam and Eve's problem wasn't only that they wanted to be like God, but also that they feared God wasn't really good and was lying to them. That is why fear is so awful. It is both the cause and the result of every spiritual "fall" that we humans endure. Fear is the fuel that keeps all addictive sin-cycles in place.

What's Driving the Car?

Emily loves everything about me except my driving (and my coffee slurping). I used to drive a sporty car and according to her I could get a little too happy with the gas, and even the brakes, while driving on the highway. Apparently riding shotgun with me wasn't that much different from riding the tilt-a-whirl at a theme park. And so in the name of becoming a better driver and husband, I did two things. First, I sold the car. My marriage improved instantly. Second, I am learning to use my cruise control. The beauty of cruise control is that you don't have to think. The car drives itself.

I do not believe that we consciously choose to live as if we were the center of the world. Judging by the vast amount of depression and unhappiness we experience, I do not think one could make the case that we even like living as mini-messiahs. Rather, I think we don't know that there are so many ways that we live our lives on cruise control. We think we are driving the car, but we are not. Fear and pride have taken the wheel.

Put differently, we all have a way that we just "be" day in and day out. We talk about our "personality" and say things like, "Well, that's just the way I am." What we often fail to see, however, is that "the way I am" is not "the way I necessarily have to be." In fact, "the way I am" is *not* the fully clothed glory self that God has already fashioned and invites us to grow into.

Christian Formation

We need to think through what our cruise control is so that we might creatively re-vision how our life might look if we knew in our bones that already we're home free. This is what growing in Christlikeness is all about. The dominant metaphor I have used to describe this process thus far is that of "new clothes." God has already given us the new wardrobe of salvation, but our new clothes do not fit. As a result our cruise control manifests itself in a commitment to lesser, shabbier loincloths that we have made for ourselves. Our imaginations must be sparked and our spirits "reborn" so that, gradually, the car we find ourselves in might turn around (the word *repent* literally means "to turn around"). This is what Christian formation, or rather Christian *re*-formation, is all about.

The goal of our faith is not action. The fruit of authentic faith might be "good works," but the goal of the Christian faith is different. Christian formation is not about doing good deeds to make God proud of us, but rather about growing into the new clothes of wholeness and love that already belong to us in and through Jesus Christ. As we "put on" love, we "take off" both fear and pride. Perfect love casts out fear, and pride is fueled by fear. Love, therefore, will always cast out pride. Fear cannot survive in the presence of love; and in the absence of fear, pride will shrivel to nothing. What this means is that rather than focusing on our actions as we seek to grow in our faith, we must focus on the inner dimensions of our personality, i.e., who we "be" as we live our lives on cruise control.

One of the best stories I have ever heard about the impotence of "good deeds" is from Tim Keller's book *The Prodigal*

God. Keller himself borrows this story from the late Charles Spurgeon.

> Once upon a time there was a gardener who grew an enormous carrot. So he took it to his king and said, "My lord, this is the greatest carrot I've ever grown or ever will grow. Therefore I want to present it to you as a token of my love and respect for you." The king was touched and discerned the man's heart, so as he turned to go the king said, "Wait! You are clearly a good steward of the earth. I own a plot of land right next to yours. I want to give it to you freely as a gift so that you can garden it all." And the gardener was amazed and delighted and went home rejoicing. But there was a nobleman at the king's court who overheard all this. And he said, "My! If that is what you get for a *carrot*—what if you gave the king something better?" So the next day the nobleman came before the king and he was leading a handsome black stallion. He bowed low and said, "My lord, I breed horses and this is the greatest horse I've ever bred or ever will. Therefore I want to present it to you as a token of my love and respect for you." But the king discerned his heart and said thank you, and took the horse and merely dismissed him. The nobleman was perplexed. So the king said, "Let me explain. That gardener was giving *me* the carrot, but you were giving your*self* the horse."[3]

The *Bigger* Why

The story is really simple, but the point is profound. The King in the story is God and the two characters represent two very

---

3 Keller, *The Prodigal God*, 69–70.

different hearts from which our "good deeds" can be performed. The question the story wants us to consider, which is the same question Jesus asks his disciples to consider, is *why?* What is our heart's motivation for doing "good" deeds?

This question is one that Jesus is very concerned with. At one point in Jesus' ministry, he notices that a lot of rich people are putting large sums into the temple treasury. Jesus then sees that a poor widow puts in a mere penny. Jesus goes out of his way to ensure that his disciples understand that it was *she,* and not the others, that gave from a heart that pleased God (Mk 12:44). In a similar manner, Jesus distinguishes between people who pray to be seen and people who pray in secret. Both groups perform the exact same action, but Jesus sees two entirely different realities flowing from two very different hearts.

This is why we need to ask the question *why*—why do we serve our God and our King? I suspect that if we are open to the truth, we will see that our cruise control setting as wounded and broken aspiring mini-messiahs is to do all things for our own gain. We are each more like the nobleman with his horse than we are the gardener with his carrot. If we are to grow out of an egocentric life, we must above all else submit our will to Jesus Christ and let Him transform us from the inside out. There is simply no other way. Jesus, in fact, is the Way.

Fear and Pride

Before we examine what a heart transformed by the grace of God looks like, it will prove beneficial to look at how fear and pride lie at the roots of our behavior. And since few would disagree that fear and pride are behind the worst of human behavior, my desire is to examine how fear and pride might also be at the root of what we call the "best" of human behavior.

We can first look at how fear motivates humans to be good. In the short run fear is a wonderful motivator and can work wonders at keeping undesired behavior in check. Any effective parent knows this. There is nothing worse than a "timeout" for a child or being grounded for a teen. It is also common to do something noble because one is afraid that otherwise he would be viewed as selfish or not particularly liked by his peers. Many Christians are obedient to God from a real fear of going to hell. These are just a few examples of how fear as a motivator for even "virtuous" human behavior is very real.

I am very present to the fear that governs my own life. My particular childhood has left me with a deep fear of abandonment. In other words, a fear of abandonment is the driving force I instinctively bring to my various relationships. The impact of this fear is that in all of my most significant relationships, my brain is moving a million miles a minute trying to process one thing: what do I need to do to keep you from leaving?

My friend Jim likes to speak of our cruise control in terms of "vows" we make. I like this language because it is so theological. As an Episcopalian I grew up making baptismal vows (we call it a baptismal covenant) to serve God. When I married Emily I made wedding vows to be a consistently loving husband. Similarly when I was ordained a priest I made a public vow in the ordination liturgy to be obedient to God and to serve all of God's children. But what my friend Jim has helped me to see is that what makes keeping these legitimate vows so darn hard is that I have also made *other* vows to protect myself and to serve the clamoring of my ego.

A vow is a decision we make, usually subconsciously as a child and usually tied to some wound, about how we need to act in this world to feel safe and avoid pain. We all make decisions about who we need to be to stay safe, in control of our destiny, and to remain pain free. This is something we all do.

I grew up with wonderful parents. My life was not more or less traumatic than the average person. But to be alive is to get hurt and to get hurt is to fear getting hurt again, and to fear getting hurt again is to learn how we must be, i.e., what cruise control *we* need to adopt, to keep us from getting hurt again. Our shields look different. But we all carry one whether we realize it or not. Good deeds can make great shields.

We need shields because of wounds that never got healed. When we were young, someone applied ointment and a bandage when we skinned our knee. But emotional and spiritual wounds are different. Our spirits get "cut" early on by nasty words, neglect, rejection, smothering, and abuse. We learn to "soldier on" and medicate those wounds ourselves. We do this by adopting a cruise control, a "personality," we think will shield us from getting hurt again. We become people-pleasers, cynics, goodie-two-shoes, rebels, performers, holy rollers, or jerks. Whether it is a good persona or a bad one, it is a persona nonetheless and a persona that is sustained by *fear.*

Like Adam and Eve before me, I have taken matters into my own hands. I fear abandonment and have made a vow to make sure no one ever leaves me: I will do whatever it takes to keep people from abandoning me. That vow is the cruise-control principle that drives my life to the extent that I am *not* living a life of prayerful reflection and striving to grow into the new clothes of salvation that *already* are mine through Jesus Christ.

We can begin to see the importance of adopting conscious Christ-centered principles that will aid us in becoming the person God says *already is.* We already have subconscious, me-centered, fear-centered principles that, whether we want to admit it or not, are really driving the car. And these me-centered, fear-centered principles exist whether we see them or not or believe in them or not. They're kind of like gravity in that way.

I invite you to wonder with me for a moment what sort of person I would be if my cruise control were to do whatever it took to avoid abandonment. If this were true, I would at the same time never appear needy, never threaten people, always appease you, be whoever you need me to be, take care of you when I am anxious or you hurt, work harder than everyone else to make sure I perform, and always seek peace over truth (to name just a few). Who does that describe? *Good, nice, well-liked, morally virtuous, hardworking, please-don't-leave, frightened-to-death ME.* In case you haven't figured this out, I am nice, sensitive, and well-liked Carl from the previous chapter, whose distaste for offending people and desire to keep the peace comes not from a place of love but from a place of fear.

I must confess that I honestly believe that God uses our wounds and the fear tied to those wounds to create virtue. We recall God's incredible skill of bringing order out of chaos. As a result of my particular wounding, I am empathetic and sensitive. And these I claim as real gifts and not simply fear-based emotional junk. As a Christian I celebrate God's grace to redeem broken experiences and bring good out of evil. However, I also know that for me to grow into Christlikeness, I must learn to be kind and sensitive not from a place of me-centered fear but rather from a place of Christ-centered love. I also believe Jesus is asking me to learn to be authentic about my needs, to be willing to exhort people I love, to live with integrity so that who I am at church is the same person I am when out with my friends. And so *what* keeps me stuck in these particular areas? The same thing, ironically, that keeps me doing all the "good" stuff. At the roots of my soul you'll find *fear.*

Pride

Just as water cannot exist without a certain concoction of hydrogen and oxygen, so too it takes both fear and *pride* for our selfish ego to survive. This is why fear is only half the problem we must deal with; the other half is pride.

The deadly, delusional disease of pride is at the heart of our Messiah complex. Pride is not a mere striving for excellence, but rather a striving to be "more excellent" than our neighbor. Pride is the ego seeking to justify itself by having more or doing more than everyone else. As C. S. Lewis put it in *Mere Christianity*, "Pride gets no pleasure out of having something, only out of having more of it than the next man." He later explains, "It is the comparison that makes you proud: the pleasure of being above the rest. Once the element of competition is gone, pride is gone."[4]

If you want to see pride at work in your heart, just notice how busy your ego always seems to be comparing itself to other people. It's not enough for us to be successful, intelligent, or good looking. No, our ego demands that we be *more* successful, *more* intelligent, or *better* looking than the next person. We are forever scanning the room to see how we measure up. And as we scan we inevitably decide whether we do or do not measure up. We all play the judge in our own case. Either we "win," which leads to bragging, or else we "fall short," which leads to contempt either for ourselves or for the other.

To see how this works in practice, consider some area of your life where you actually feel you "excel" (a kind way of saying an area where you feel superior to other people). In this case, comparing leads to "winning" and winning leads to bragging. Of course we may not brag out loud, but our ego is built up as we take inner delight in being the best in some arena that the world values. We recall Jesus' parable of the Pharisee and tax collector. "God, I thank you that I am not like other people: thieves, rogues, adulterers, or even like this tax collector. I fast twice a week; I give a tenth of all my income" (Lk 18:11–12). This Pharisee built an identity or sense of self on being more pious than other men and in his own eyes he succeeded. What makes pride so deadly and delusional is that it blinds us. What this Pharisee failed to see, and what we often fail to see, is that we *are* like other men. In fact, all of us are the exact same! Me, you, Hitler, John the murderer, the grocer at the market—we

---

4 Lewis, *Mere Christianity*, 122.

all fall short, live lives buried in an avalanche of addiction, and need rescue from the outside. The Pharisee built his identity around his own moral strivings. The tax collector, on the other hand, stole his sense of worth from gaining wealth. But *both* were building an identity around something other than God. Spiritual bragging is cancer. As Paul exhorted the Corinthians, "Your boasting is not . . . good!" (1 Cor 5:6). Now that's an understatement if I've ever heard one.

But we don't always come out on top after comparing ourselves with others. We sometimes see gifts or social graces in others that we ourselves do not possess and our instinctual response is to feel contempt. We're not good at school, at preaching, or at getting the girls. We're not athletic, rich, or good in large groups. And so what do we do? We show contempt. To have contempt means to deem someone or something as less than. And because our ego's main desire is to look good (or at least not bad), to win (or at least not lose), to finish first (or at least not last), whenever we compare ourselves to some person or some standard and fall short, it *always* leads to contempt.

Falling short is often felt as contempt for ourselves. *I'm such an idiot.* Self-hate talk, excessive guilt, and feelings of unworthiness all have their roots, ironically, in our pride. Or, we can feel contempt for someone else. *She's pretty yeah, but what an airhead.* I believe that feeling contempt for others is harder to see than contempt for ourselves because it takes more forms. We make excuses, we gossip, we get cynical, we blame, we experience anger. But at the roots of these behaviors you'll always find contempt. The ego that wants nothing more than to win has lost, and because it can't make itself taller the only remaining option is to make someone or something else smaller. There is much more to be written about the adverse effects of fear and pride on the human heart, but suffice it to say that fear and pride are at the root of our, as Alcoholics Anonymous puts it, "unmanageable lives."

My hope here has been to establish just how infected the human heart truly is at its root so as to demonstrate how any measures we take to "tidy it up" simply will not do. There is a big difference between restraining the heart and changing the heart, and the latter of the two is the only option Jesus gives us. "Behold," He says, "I make all things new" (see Rev 21:5).

A New Heart

This book is about spiritual growth or transformation or maturity or whatever words *you* prefer to describe the practice of putting on the "new clothes" of salvation that already belong to us in Jesus Christ. To elucidate this theme further, we need to see that at the heart of such spiritual transformation is a completely new heart that God longs to give to each one of us. The natural condition of our heart, as Jeremiah notes, is "devious above all else" and "perverse" (Jer 17:9). The prophet then goes on to explain that a day is coming when God will write His law on our hearts (Jer 31:33). Ezekiel goes as far as to say that God will give us a completely "new heart" (Ez 36:26). As Jesus himself noted, it is the cruise control of the human heart in its present state that accounts for all of humanity's problems (Mk 7:21). Thus it is our fear and pride-infected hearts, or what I have also referred to as our *spirit-drives,* that must change.

Our world's great need and our church's great need and our marriage's great need is *not* better education, better technology, the right curriculum, or even a reminder that we need to try harder. "There is need of only one thing" (Lk 10:42). We must learn to sit at the feet of Jesus and cultivate the habit of letting the Master Surgeon do his fitting and proper work on our hearts. We need to commit ourselves to the lifelong process of acquiring God's heart.

Of course the key word here is "process." Like all things worthwhile in life, growth in the spiritual life is a process and a journey. The journey has peaks and valleys. Sometimes the journey is dull and sometimes it is really exciting. We sometimes feel close to God and He sometimes seems far away. Like Israel's experience in the wilderness after the Exodus, we have "Red Sea" moments and moments when water miraculously gushes forth from a rock. There are perhaps even more "golden calf" moments and "I've been at the same place for forty years and I am bored and cynical!" moments. In keeping with this metaphor, it is a long journey to the "Promised Land," i.e., to the dawning of God's new world where we will fully don the garment of salvation and dance before Jesus being perfect and complete "without a spot or wrinkle or anything of the kind" (Eph 5:27). We can't lose sight of the fact that we will not fully experience God's new world before we die (though it *is* mysteriously already fully here), for without a belief in the future of God's new world, we will lose hope along the way. This of course raises the question: if the process of change is long and slow, what will sustain us on our journey?

Beauty or Duty?

There are only two forces that can sustain a Christian in the wonderful, awesome, frustrating, all-consuming task of being consumed by Jesus' grace and transformed deeper into His likeness: *beauty* and *duty*.

I fear that when most people imagine a "faithful Christian," they see a person committed above all else to an inner sense of duty that compels them to act morally superior to others. But if we read the gospels carefully, Jesus never appealed to our sense of duty, nor did he ever give a lecture on the importance of doing the right thing. In fact, Jesus never said, "I am here to help you find God." Not once. What Jesus said was, "I am God. I am here to find you." Jesus' teaching was geared at opening human hearts to a new possibility that we might share in God's own life and reign in His Kingdom through a life of service and love. In other words, Jesus' strategy was not to help us learn to restrain our heart, but to change it by giving the human heart something exceedingly beautiful to pursue: Himself.

One of the things I love about the Episcopal Church is our liturgy. If you've never been to an Episcopal Church, I would encourage you to go at least once and to pay close attention to what you hear prayed in the liturgy. One of the things you will note is that a sense of delight, joy, praise, and thanksgiving infuses our worship. For example, in our confession we ask God to forgive our sins so that "we might delight" in God's will (BCP, 360). In our Baptismal liturgy we pray that the newest members of Christ's Body will receive the gift of "joy and wonder" (308). And in our Eucharist we are crystal clear that the only sacrifice God wants from His people is one of "praise and thanksgiving" (369).

It is fitting that words like delight, joy, praise, and thanksgiving are used throughout the Episcopal liturgy. According to the Bible, they are the fuel that sustains a disciple's life. Duty is a bucket of water poured on the fire of the disciple's life. Beauty, on the other hand, is like "precious oil" poured out (Ps 133:2). The oil of God's beauty is what sets a fire ablaze in our heart. Only the beauty of who Christ is will keep the fire of our devotion burning so that the light of our faith will naturally "shine before others" (Mt 5:16).

Our life will never shine from a sense of duty or obligation because they are both sustained themselves by the twin cancers of fear and pride. Such is why authentic Christianity is not about doing our duty, but rather about delight, love, joy, and praise that overflow into good works. Our life of inner transformation into Christlikeness is sustained only when we are committed to seeing the beauty of God.

The Power of the Gospel

In his letter to the church at Rome, St. Paul says something that has revolutionized how I see the Christian life. He writes, "I am not ashamed of the gospel; it is the power of God for salvation to everyone who has faith" (Rom 1:16). Paul has gotten to a place in his own life before God that he is not ashamed of the Gospel. I am not sure whether I am fully there yet or not. Part of me might still be ashamed. If one does not understand why one *might* be ashamed of the Christian Gospel, I would question whether they ever understood the Gospel in the first place. It's a shameful story where the Tall God of creation became quite small so that we, who puff about life fearfully trying to stand taller than one another, might be made quite small indeed.

Now I know that sounds harsh, but we do well to remember that the word gospel means "good news." Paul then goes on to say that this "good news" is itself a power for those who believe. It is important here to remind ourselves that the word "believe" means to trust in a living Person, not to intellectually assent to church dogma. Now obviously so much of our dogma comes from what Jesus taught and so let us not assume, as many often do, that we are more informed than Jesus in such matters. But faith is not about conforming to doctrine; it is about conforming to Christ's likeness. This inner transformation only happens to the extent that we begin deriving our sense of worth from *Him,* and begin building our identity on what He has done for us and what He says about us.

So much of what keeps the fear and pride driving the car is that we are always trying to find our worth and our deepest identity in a million places other than God. Perhaps it is our spouse, our job, our I.Q., our performance, our children's performance. It can be anything really. Donald Miller tells the story of how depressed a bearded woman got when a three-legged man joined her circus. Before he came along she had always been the top-grossing act. Her worth had always been tied to being the biggest freak and now there was a bigger freak at the circus. And so if not the biggest freak, who was she now? That was her question.[5]

I am not trying to be crass, but the vast majority of the questions we ask in life, in light of the Christian Gospel, can sound just as foolish. We scatter about trying to steal a sense of worth when all along the King of Creation whispers in a still small voice: *"What are you doing? You are my treasured possession! Stop. Live for Me. I've got meaningful work for you to do! I'll take care of you. But live for Me. Your worth lies in what I've done for you and what I say about you. You're my child!"*

This is the good news that God speaks to each and every one of us, and it is powerful news. Only to the extent that we are creatively and consistently rooting our lives in this good news and being smitten by its beauty can we give the King the carrot, metaphorically speaking, from a place of joy and love, and not fear and pride.

When Fear and Pride Are Crucified

The Gospel is not something we ever outgrow. In fact, as we grow spiritually, the Gospel is that which we habitually and intentionally *re*-turn to through a life of prayerful reflection in the context of an authentic community. The word "repent" simply means to turn, and re-turning to the good news of the new person we already are in Christ is not something we ever stop doing. Only Jesus can clothe us in Himself as we habitually have our mind renewed with the grace-full news of who we are in Him. Such is why spiritual disciplines like praying, giving, fasting, bible reading, and any other spiritual practice we take on are not ways that we make ourselves worthy so that we might stand

---

5 Miller tells this story in *Searching for God Knows What* (Nashville, TN: Thomas Nelson, 2010). The title of chapter 11 is, "A Circus of Redemption: Why a Three-Legged Man Is Better than a Bearded Woman."

before God, but rather ways that we turn, again and again and again, to the life-transforming truth that God has already made us worthy to stand before Him. A spiritual discipline properly understood is anything that further converts our heart to the truth that God already has made us His treasure.

And as we re-turn to the Truth, we find that slowly but surely God removes the roots of fear and pride that govern so much of our behavior. For instance, consider for a moment what sort of person you would be if your heart knew that, in order to save you, God emptied Himself, took the form of a slave, and died on the cross in your place so that you could share in God's own life. Ponder for a moment what your life would be like if this belief was as real to your heart as the belief that the sun would rise tomorrow or that gravity were a real force in our world. If this were the case, pride of any sort would be psychologically impossible. If we truly believed that we were so addicted to ourselves that Christ died to liberate us and that we were instinctively "evil" as Jesus Himself said (Lk 11:13), any form of pride or self-righteousness would be a psycholog-ical impossibility. I would posit that the reason we often live as stubborn children that pout, condemn, and gossip whenever our will is crossed is because our heart does not believe that Christ died for *us*. Christ may have died for the world in general or for the jerk that cut me off this morning, but surely God did not have to become small and die for me! If it is indeed true that God became human and died for me, it must also be true that there is absolutely no room for pride.

On the other hand, we might wonder whether the Gospel of Jesus' death on our behalf leaves any room for fear or shame. I emphatically insist that it does not! After all, the reason God chose to save us is because His love for us is so great! The cross reveals just how far God is willing to go to lavish His love onto us. It shows that God promises never to leave us or abandon us. The cross emphatically insists that God has paid every moral debt we could ever accrue and more, and that God's deepest desire is to call us His child. As we look at the cross, our heart must shout "how loved are we!" I believe that only as our hearts begin to understand God's amazing love for us made concrete in Jesus' crucifixion will all fear gradually be cast out.

Humility and Boldness: An Unlikely Pairing

The impact of all that has been said thus far is that whenever we speak of a uniquely Christian spirituality, we are talking about growing in two practical graces that conventional wisdom says cannot co-exist but that Jesus insists must go together in we who bear His name. One of these virtues is humility and the other is boldness.

On the one hand, as Jesus' heart comes to replace ours, we become more humble. We get very present to the truth that God had to die in order to save us. We slowly but surely grasp that Christianity is not about our goodness or our achievements, but rather about God's goodness and God's unwavering commitment to save us. Such is why the Gospel is a power that humbles us. The Gospel keeps us small.

But on the other hand, the Christian Gospel makes us bold, which must be distinguished from arrogance. There is a confidence and boldness that arises out of knowing just how secure we are in Christ. As one wise elder rightly understood, "The righteous are as bold as a lion" (Prov 28:1). In fact, growing in boldness must happen as we come to know that the God of the universe knows our name and that He died to "clothe" us with God's own life (see 2 Cor 5:4).

This is precisely why St. Paul says the Gospel is a *power.* Indeed, the Gospel is the only power for transformation that Christianity offers. For only in the light of the Gospel do we see that we are more broken than we ever quite understood and more loved than we ever dared imagine. This produces within us a bold humility, which is no doubt a uniquely Christian pairing that brings us deeper and deeper into the life of God. As Eugene Peterson puts it, "Humble boldness (or, bold humility) enters into a sane, robust willing—free willing—and finds its most expressive and satisfying experience in prayer to Jesus Christ, who wills our salvation."[6]

The Power of Stories

A word I haven't used very often is *story*. We recall from earlier that something only has an identity in a particular context. Another way of saying that is that there is no "me" apart from a particular story where "I" exist as a character.

Stories tell us who we are, what to value, and what gives us worth. I would posit that the vast majority of pain in life arises out of humanity's (mostly unconscious) insistence on living some story *other* than the Christian Gospel. I wrote this book so that we all might ponder just exactly what story *we* are rooting our lives in.

Not all stories are created equal. Part of becoming an emotionally mature human being is taking conscious responsibility for what our story with a capital "S" is going to be. Upon deciding, we must take responsibility for consistently rooting our lives and souls in whatever story we choose. I write from a deep belief that the Christian story is THE story. As the late Brennan Manning once put it, history is really His-Story.

My hope is that you will cultivate the habit of seeing the many counter-stories that threaten to rob us of the abundant life that Jesus offers us and re-turn, as often as it takes, to the Main Character of THE only story that has the power to make us whole.

Perhaps this means walking away from a family story you inherited. Perhaps you grew up hearing and believing things like, "I am proud of you *when* you make all A's. If a stranger

---

6 Eugene Peterson, *The Contemplative Pastor* (Grand Rapids, MI: Wm. B. Eerdmans Publishing, 1993), 109.

knocks, don't answer the door. We don't associate with people that live *there*." Or maybe it is the cultural stories that most threaten to choke your faith. Perhaps you believe life is all about "obeying your thirst." Or maybe your sense of self is rooted in how you look or how much money you make or how often you're getting laid or some other cultural, consumerist value. Or, perhaps the trickiest of all, religious stories have taken hold of your heart. I would counsel you that the vast majority of religious stories are actually anathema to the Christian Gospel. These stories ooze out in phrases like, "God helps people who help themselves," and "why would God let this happen to me, I haven't done anything wrong?"

The point is there are all types of stories that clamor for our allegiance and faith. But then there is THE Story, which we call the Christian Gospel. And this Gospel story is a power that is uniquely equipped to transform us into boldly humble friends of Jesus. The point of life is for this story to become *our* story with a capital "S." We must come to trust in this Gospel story to the same extent that we trust in gravity's reality.

Wrapping It Up

I would like to return to the beginning. We recall that Adam and Eve "fell," at least in part, because they wanted to be "like God." It would be wrong to assume that our desire to be "like" God is really our problem. Our great problem is always our failure to understand what God is actually "like." The power of the Gospel is that it reveals to us what God *is* actually "like" and what it would mean for us to be more "like" Him. This is how St. Paul puts it in Philippians 2:5–7:

> Let the same mind be in you that was in Christ Jesus, who, though he was in the form of God, did not regard equality with God as something to be exploited, but emptied himself, taking the form of a slave.

It is absolutely crucial that we understand what Paul is saying about God. We often assume that Paul is saying that Jesus took the form of a slave in spite of the fact that he was God. In other words, Jesus was God, but he took the form of a slave anyway. But what Paul is saying, if you read the Greek carefully, is that Jesus took the form of a slave precisely *because* he was God. God's choice to become human and die for us doesn't disguise who God really is, nor does Jesus' life and death disguise God's true nature. On the contrary, God's choice to become human and to die for us reveals who God really is. God becoming small isn't a disguise. Do you see how radical this is? What Paul is saying is that the God we worship, and the Lord we're invited to follow, is humble.

My hope is that you hunger at a deep level to be transformed in the very depths of your soul. Take comfort in the knowledge that this very desire is evidence that the process of your rebirth has indeed begun and that He who began this work in you, i.e., God Himself, will bring it to completion by the Day when God's new world dawns once and for all (Phil 1:6). What this means, practically speaking, is that your "work" is to re-turn, over and over again, to the truth that the God we worship and the Lord we are invited to follow is humble. He became small for *you*.

Only to the extent that we believe that God became human to serve us will we find the security, self-confidence, and worth that we've been looking for all our lives. For in Christ, God offers us a security and a self-confidence that comes not from making ourselves the center, but from knowing that in Christ, God has made us the center of His life.

Christianity, at the end of the day, is nothing less than a big, fat, funny, and powerfully true paradox. We grow up as we learn to grow down. The higher place is found in taking the lower one. We live only as we die. We become spiritual adults only as we change and become like children. We enter *into* Him to find ourselves. His Story becomes our unique history. We learn who we are only as we experience that HE IS *the big why*.

Is this THE story you are rooting your life in? Jesus' invitation is the same today as it was two thousand years ago. "Come to me, all you that are weary and are carrying heavy burdens, and I will give you rest. Take my yoke upon you, and learn from me; for I am gentle and humble in heart, and you will find rest for your souls." In other words, each one of us is invited into a personal, lifelong, growing relationship with the only person in human history who never suffered from a Messiah complex. And this person just happens to be the Messiah himself, around whom the world does truly revolve. And as we grow in the Messiah and the Messiah grows in us, the snake's words to Eve will prove ironically true: our eyes will be opened, and we will be like God.

Discussion Questions

1. How would you define pride? How would you define fear? What is the relationship between the two?

2. Do you think fear and pride often motivate even our *good works?*

3. What does it mean to say we're all an aspiring "mini-Messiah"? Do you agree with this statement?

4. What "persona" have you adopted to protect yourself? Can you identify any specific wounds that may have led you to form that persona?

5. Some describe the spiritual life as a journey where we never fully arrive. Does this idea frustrate you or excite you? Do you agree that we *never* "arrive?"

6. Is it possible to grow in humility and boldness at the same time?

7. Do you believe God is humble? Can God be humble *and* all-powerful at the same time?

Epilogue: One Thing

In the 1991 film *City Slickers,* Billy Crystal plays a confused and dissatisfied middle-aged salesman named Mitch. Mitch has this vague sense that life is passing him by. He's not completely sure what he's living for anymore, and so Mitch goes on a cattle drive with two of his friends in the hope of finding some clarity led by a cowboy named Curly. At one point in the movie, Curly asks Mitch if he would like to know the secret of life.

"It's this," Curly says, holding up a single finger. Mitch gets uncomfortable and resorts to sarcasm. "The secret of life is your finger?" he asks. "It's one thing," Curly replies. "The secret of life is pursuing one thing."

I agree with Curly. Curly, of course, stole this life secret from Jesus. We recall the words Jesus once spoke to a confused and dissatisfied middle-aged homemaker named Martha: "there is need of only *one thing*" (Lk 10:42, italics mine).

I believe there is only "one thing" worth pursuing in life—a heart transformed from the inside out by the grace and mercy of Jesus Christ. Throughout this book I have used the metaphor of "new clothes" to describe the renewed heart God wants to give us—the salvation we *already have* but that, at present, does not yet fully fit us. I wish now to leave you with one last image, the story of Eustace's transformation in C. S. Lewis' *The Voyage of the Dawn Treader.*

In Lewis' story the young man Eustace wakes up one morning to discover that he has become a dragon. Eustace's hardened and grotesque dragon skin is a metaphor for Eustace's hardened and grotesque character. Lewis has consistently portrayed Eustace as selfish and nasty. Eventually Eustace sees himself as the dragon that he has become and he wants more than anything to become a boy again. But Eustace knows that he needs help. He simply cannot shed his dragon skin alone.

It is in his despair that Eustace meets the great lion Aslan, who represents Christ in Lewis' *Chronicles of Narnia*. Aslan leads Eustace to a well and tells him to undress so that Eustace might bathe in the water. So Eustace peels off a layer of his dragon skin. At first Eustace feels better, but he quickly notices there is more dragon skin to peel off! And so Eustace continues to peel off his dragon skin. But with each layer of dragon skin he peels off, Eustace finds another scaly layer of dragon skin under it. Eustace makes no progress in undressing himself and wonders in frustration how many layers he must peel! The lion Aslan then explains that *He* must be the one to undress Eustace. This is how Lewis captures Eustace's reaction:

I was afraid of his claws, I can tell you, but I was pretty nearly desperate now. So I just lay flat down on my back and let him do it. The very first tear he made was so deep that I thought it had gone right into my heart. And when he began pulling the skin off, it hurt worse than anything I've ever felt. The only thing that made me able to bear it was just the pleasure of feeling the stuff peel off . . . Well, he peeled the beastly stuff right off—just as I thought I'd done it myself the other three times, only they hadn't hurt—and there it was lying on the grass: only ever so much thicker, and darker, and more knobbly-looking than the others had been. And there I was as smooth and soft as a peeled switch and smaller than I had been. Then he caught hold of me—I didn't like that much for I was very tender underneath now that I'd no skin on—and threw me into the water. It smarted like anything but only for a moment. After that it became perfectly delicious and as soon as I started swimming and splashing I found that all the pain had gone from my arm. And then I saw why. I'd turned into a boy again . . . After a bit the lion took me out and dressed me."[1]

At this point Edmund, to whom Eustace is recounting the story, interrupts. "Dressed you. With his paws?" "Well, I don't exactly remember that bit," Eustace replied. "But he did somehow or the other: *in new clothes.*"

Lewis' tale of Eustace's transformation captures the "one thing" God invites all of us to experience. We have covered ourselves in scaly loincloths of our own making. They are so much a part of our identity that shedding them will make us feel worse before we start to feel better. But the good news of the Christian Gospel is *that we are invited to bathe in the waters of our baptism and become children once again.* "And unless you [do]," Jesus once said, "you will never enter the kingdom of heaven" (Mt 18:3).

---

1 C. S. Lewis, *The Voyage of the Dawn Treader: The Chronicles of Narnia, Book 5* (New York: Harper Collins, 1952/2008), 109–110.

Works Cited

Achtemeier, Paul. *Romans*. Louisville, KY: John Knox Press, 1985.

Augustine. *Confessions of Saint Augustine*.

Barth, Karl. *Church Dogmatics III.2: The Doctrine of Creation*. New York: T & T Clark International, 2004.

Bradshaw, John. *Healing the Shame That Binds You*. Deerfield Beach, FL: Health Communications, Inc., 1988.

Brown, Brené. *The Gifts of Imperfection: Let Go of Who You Think You're Supposed to Be and Embrace Who You Are*. Center City, MN: Hazelden, 2010.

Elkins, David. *Beyond Religion: A Personal Program for Building a Spiritual Life Outside the Walls of Traditional Religion*. Wheaton, IL: Quest Books, 1998.

Foster, Richard. *Prayer: Finding the Heart's True Home*. New York: HarperCollins, 1992.

Friedman, Edwin. *A Failure of Nerve*. New York: Seabury, 2007.

Heschel, Abraham. *The Prophets*. New York: Harper & Row, 1962.

Keller, Timothy J. *The Prodigal God: Recovering the Heart of the Christian Faith*. New York: Penguin Group, 2008.

Keller, Timothy J. *The Reason for God: Belief in an Age of Skepticism*. New York: Dutton, 2008.

Kierkegaard, Søren. *The Sickness Unto Death: A Christian Psychological Exposition for Upbuilding and Awakening*. 1849.

Lewis, C. S. *Mere Christianity*. San Francisco: HarperSanFrancisco, 1952.

Lewis, C. S. *The Voyage of the Dawn Treader: The Chronicles of Narnia, Book 5*. New York: HarperCollins, 1952/2008.

McLaren, Brian and Tony Campolo. *Adventures in Missing the Point: How the Culture-Controlled Church Neutered the Gospel*. Grand Rapids, MI: Zondervan, 2003.

Merton, Thomas. *Disputed Questions*. The Trustees of the Thomas Merton Legacy Trust, 1988.

Merton, Thomas. *New Seeds of Contemplation*. New York: New Directions Publishing Corp., 1961.

Miller, Donald. *Searching for God Knows What*. Nashville, TN: Thomas Nelson, 2010.

Nouwen, Henri. *In the Name of Jesus* (New York: Crossroad, 1992), 24.

Nouwen, Henri. *Lifesigns: Intimacy, Fecundity, and Ecstasy in Christian Perspective.* New York: Doubleday, 1986.

Nouwen, Henri. *Reaching Out: The Three Movements of the Spiritual Life.* New York: Doubleday, 1975.

Ortberg, John. *The Life You Have Always Wanted: Spiritual Disciplines for Ordinary People.* Grand Rapids, MI: Zondervon, 1997.

Peterson, Eugene. *Five Smooth Stones for Pastoral Work.* Grand Rapids, MI: Eerdmans Publishing Company, 1992.

Peterson, Eugene. *The Contemplative Pastor.* Grand Rapids, MI: Wm. B. Eerdmans Publishing, 1993.

Rollins, Peter. *The Fidelity of Betrayal: Towards a Church Beyond Belief.* Brewster, MA: Paulist Press, 2008.

Smith, James Bryan. *The Good and Beautiful God: Falling in Love with the God Jesus Knows.* Downer's Grove, IL: InterVarsity Press, 2009.

Stott, John. *The Cross of Christ.* Downers Grove, IL: Intervarsity Press, 2006.

Sullivan, Andrew. "The Forgotten Jesus." *Newsweek* (April 9, 2012).

Willard, Dallas. *The Divine Conspiracy: Rediscovering Our Hidden Life in God.* San Francisco: Harper, 1998.

Willard, Dallas. *Renovation of the Heart: Putting on the Character of Christ.* Colorado Springs, CO: NavPress, 2002.

Willard, Dallas. *The Great Omission: Reclaiming Jesus's Essential Teachings on Discipleship.* Oxford, UK: Monarch Books, 2006.

Wright, N. T. *After You Believe: Why Christian Character Matters.* New York: HarperCollins, 2010.

Wright, N. T. *Simply Christian: Why Christianity Makes Sense.* New York: HarperCollins, 2006.